R R R

Note for Librarians: A cataloguing record for this book is available from Library and Archives Canada at www.collectionscanada.ca/amicus/index-e.html
ISBN 1-4251-0288-3

Offices in Canada, USA, Ireland and UK

Book sales for North America and international:
Trafford Publishing, 6E–2333 Government St.,
Victoria, BC V8T 4P4 CANADA
phone 250 383 6864 (toll-free 1 888 232 4444)
fax 250 383 6804; email to orders@trafford.com
Book sales in Europe:
Trafford Publishing (UK) Limited, 9 Park End Street, 2nd Floor
Oxford, UK OX1 1HH UNITED KINGDOM
phone 44 (0)1865 722 113 (local rate 0845 230 9601)
facsimile 44 (0)1865 722 868; info.uk@trafford.com
Order online at:
trafford.com/06-2045

10 9 8 7 6 5 4 3 2 1

RHYME

REASON

REVERENCE

By

Estella Davis

Contents

PREFACE

IF YOU ARE ONE OF THE BILLIONS OF MEMBERS OF THE HUMAN RACE, YOU ARE WELL AWARE THAT IT WILL TAKE MORE THAN JUST FIVE OR TEN YEARS INTO THE NEW MILLENNIUM TO EVEN GET ACQUAINTED WITH SOME OF THE CHANGES HERALD BY THE NEW CENTURY.

ONE IMPORTANT THING TO REMEMBER IS THAT BEING A MEMBER OF THE HUMAN RACE PUTS US IN A VERY UNIQUE CLASS OF INDIVIDUALS. WE ARE THE ONLY SPECIES THAT TALK AS A MODE OF COMMUNICATION, HENCE, WE CAN CONVERSE, INTELLIGENTLY. WE ARE THE ONLY SPECIES THAT UTILIZES WORDS AS A WAY OF TRANSLATING OUR THOUGHTS, INTENTIONS OR ABILITIES. ALL OF CREATION COMMUNICATE, BUT, NONE LIKE THE HUMAN RACE.

SO, WE WANT TO REMEMBER THAT, AS WE OBSERVE THE ROADS, BEING PAVED FOR FURTHER TECHNOLOGY IN THE TWENTY-FIRST CENTURY. TALKING, SPEAKING WITH WORDS THROUGH PRINT, SCRIPT, MOTION, SONG, PICTURE AND PERSONALLY WILL STILL KEEP US IN THE CATEGORY THAT IS ONLY OCCUPIED BY THE HUMAN RACE. THEN AND ONLY THEN IS ADVANCEMENT REALLY ADVANCEMENT AND PROGRESS, REALLY PROGRESS.

WITH THIS IN MIND, WE UNDERSTAND WHAT THE TERM, "THE WORD OF GOD" MEANS. THEN WE KNOW THE IMPORTANCE OF WORDS LIKE, 'RHYME', 'REASON' AND 'REVERENCE'.

FOREWORD

IT IS MY DESIRE TO LEND A LITTLE CREDENCE TO THE BELIEF THAT SHARING CAN BE BENEFICIAL TO, BOTH, THE SHAREE AND THE SHARER. THERE IS NO MALICIOUS INTENT ASSOCIATED WITH THE WRITING, EDITING, COMPILATION, PRINTING PUBLISHING OR MARKETING OF "RHYME, REASON & REVERENCE".

IT HAS BEEN MY EXPERIENCE THAT PEOPLE CAN APPRECIATE THE EFFORT BEHIND PERSONAL ENDEAVORS TO SHOW THAT LITERARY FIELDS, FOR BOTH, READERS AND AUTHORS ARE, INDEED, TWO-WAY STREETS, PAVED WITH, BOTH, CRITICISM AND ACCEPTANCE. BUT, THE WORTH IS, ULTIMATELY, IN THE SENSE OF SATISFACTION WE GET FROM AVENUES AVAILABLE TO US AS WAYS TO ILLUSTRATE OUR IDEAS,THOUGHTS AND VISIONS FOR YEARS TO COME, HOPEFULLY, HELPING TO PRESENT POSITIVE FOCUS FOR READERS AND WRITERS OF TOMORROW.

INTRODUCTION

THE WAR WILL BE OVER ONE DAY AND THE IRAQI PEOPLE AND THE MUSLIM WORLD WILL BE VIEWING THINGS IN A DIFFERENT LIGHT AS WILL THE AMERICAN PEOPLE.

WARS ARE FOUGHT FOR DIFFERENT REASONS, AS ANY PARTICIPANT OR OBSERVER WILL ATTEST. THEY ARE, SOMETIMES, FOUGHT BY MEN, OTHER TIMES THEY ARE FOUGHT BY NATIONS, STILL, OTHER TIMES WARS ARE FOUGHT BY WORLDS OR GODS IN WHAT IS CALLED PRINCIPALITIES AND HIGH PLACES.

REASONING WILL PRECLUDE ANY AGREEMENT THAT LEADS TO LASTING PEACE. THIS CAN, ONLY HAPPEN WHEN THE WAR OF THE WORLDS AND GODS SUBMIT TO THE APPEAL OF THE NATIONS AS THEY TRULY REALIZE THAT ONE MAN, ONE VOTE AND ONE NATION UNDER GOD IS NOT ONLY A WAY TO PEACE AND LATER FREEDOM, BUT, IT IS CONSIDERED THE ONE AND ONLY WAY TO LASTING PEACE BY MANY NATIONS AND THEIR PEOPLE.

WARS, TRAGEDIES AND UNREST AMONG PEOPLE ACROSS THE COUNTRY AND THE WORLD IS NOT NEW TO SOME OF US AND IS CONSIDERED TO BE BORING AND JUST MORE 'MUCH ADO ABOUT NOTHING'. STILL, OTHERS FIND IT VERY INTERESTING THAT PEOPLE WOULD PROFESS LOVE AS EVERYTHING, BUT, FIND IT A LESSER CALLING THAN THE CALL TO ARMS. IT IS ALL SO PERPLEXING AND SCHIZOID TO MANY OF US.

RATHER THAN BORING A READER WITH THE SAME OLD HUM-DRUM THAT DESCRIBES OUR COUNTRY AND WORLD'S UNREST, I CHOSE TO TRY TO CONNECT THE DOTS, SO TO SPEAK, IN AN ELEMENTARY SORT OF WAY TO MARK CURRENT EVENTS THAT ARE SURE TO BECOME HISTORICAL AT SOME TIME IN THE FUTURE.

I WOULD HOPE THAT THE BOOK WOULD BE INSPIRING TO SOME, INFORMATIVE TO OTHERS AND MAYBE, EVEN, HELPFUL TO OTHER READERS. SOME OF THE EVENTS UNFOLDED, ALREADY IN THE TWENTY-FIRST CENTURY LEADS US TO THINK THAT THIS CENTURY WILL, INDEED, BE A MEMORABLE AND REMARKABLE TIME IN THE FUTURE THAT WOULD DO, ANYTHING, BUT, ALLOW US TO FORGET THE PEOPLE AND EVENTS OF THE TWENTIETH CENTURY.

THERE IS SAID TO BE A TELEPHONE DIRECTORY, A DICTIONARY AND A RECIPE BOOK IN EVERY LITERATE HOUSEHOLD. I WOULD HOPE THAT YOU WOULD ADD TO THAT, A HAND-BOOD OF INSPIRATION, DEDICATION, MEMORY AND THOUGHT. IT IS WITH THIS IN MIND THAT RHYME - REASON - REFERENCE IS WRITTEN AND PUPLISHED.

THE AUTHOR/PUBLISHER

DEDICATION

THIS BOOK IS DEDICATED TO
THOSE WITH A MEMORY OF THE PAST,
A MIND OF THE PRESENT AND A
DREAM OF THE FUTURE.

Part 1

"I AM MAD AS HELL" NETWORK

"I ONLY WISH WE WERE IN THE ARMY" BLIND DATE

"FOR GOD'S SAKE, LET HIM DROP THE BOMB" HANOVER STREET

"PLAY IT AGAIN, SAM" CASABLANCA

"DON'T CALL ME PROFESSOR, CALL ME SHERMAN" THE NUTTY PROFESSOR

"YOU CAN'T HANDLE THE TRUTH" A FEW GOOD MEN

DREAMING DREAMS

DID YOU EVER HAVE A DREAM
WHERE YOU WERE FULLY AWAKE
BUT, ASLEEP, FULLY ASLEEP?

YES, BECAUSE IN
THIS DREAM, I WAS
AWAKE IN MY SLEEP
AND ASLEEP IN MY BED,
THE FUNNY THING
ABOUT IT WAS
THE DREAM SEEMED
TO LAST FOR HOURS.

BUT, ALL I DID
IN THIS DREAM
WHERE I WAS WIDE
AWAKE IN MY SLEEP
IN MY BED

WAS TRY TO WAKE UP.

EMD

ON A CLEAR DAY
WE CAN SEE FOREVER
THOUGH CHASING RAINBOWS
MIGHT BE MORE CLEVER.

EMD

WHAT HAPPENS WHEN YOU LOVE SOMETHING?

IF IT'S A BIRD, YOU LET FLY AWAY
IF IT'S A ROCK, YOU LET IT BECOME
A BOULDER
IF IT'S A CATERPILLER, YOU ALLOW
METAMORPHISIS
IF IT'S A DAY, YOU WILL YEILD
TO THE NIGHT
IF IT'S A FERRIS WHEEL, YOU WILL
LET IT GO ROUND AND ROUND
IF IT'S A FISH, YOU WILL LET IT SWIM
IF IT'S A ROSEBUD, YOU WILL
WAIT FOR THE BLOSSOM
IF IT'S A SEE-SAW, YOU WILL
LET IT GO UP AND DOWN
IF IT'S AN EVERGREEN YOU
WILL ALLOW PHOTOSYNTHESIS
IF IT'S A BEAUTIFUL PIECE OF ART,
YOU WILL HANG IT FOR ALL TO SEE
IF IT WAS AN UMBRELLA, YOU'D
LET IT SHIELD MANY FROM THE RAIN
IF IT WAS AN ICE CREAM CONE,
YOU WOULD CHOOSE A BERRY FLAVOR
IF IT WAS A GERM YOU WOULD
HURRY TO CATCH A COLD
BUT, IF IT WAS ME, I'D LET YOU KNOW
THAT NOTHING GOOD LASTS FOREVER
AND LOVE IS GOOD AND PARTING IS
SUCH SWEET SORROW.

EMD

A WEEK FULL

MONDAYS FIND ME, BLUE
TUESDAYS, SPIRITS, HIGH
WEDNESDAYS, SKIES, I MEET
THURSDAYS, I PEACEFUL, FALL
FRIDAYS, ALL PUFFED UP
SATURDAYS, PLAYTIME, PLENTY
SUNDAYS, BLESSED BY IT ALL.

EMD

THE PARADOX OF LIFE

THE RISING AND THE
SETTING OF THE SUN

THE RINGING OF DINNER
AND SCHOOL BELLS

THE WITNESS OF THE RAIN
THE HEAT OF THE DESERT

TO GRADUATE, ONLY
TO COMMENCE AGAIN

TO ASCEND, ONLY
TO DESCEND, MORE

LIFE IS FULL OF PARADOXES
THE PARADOX OF LIFE.

EMD

IN JANUARY, I RESOLVED TO
BE A BETTER PERSON

IN FEBRUARY, I DANCED TO
MY HEART'S CONTENT

IN MARCH, I PRAISED
THE WIND FOR IT'S BREEZE

IN APRIL, I SMELLED
FLOWERS THAT HEAVEN SENT.

IN MAY, I REMEMBERED
TO PLANT YELLOW ROSES

IN JUNE, I COULD FEEL
ESSENCE OF BIRDS-TO-BE

IN JULY, I TASTED SIMPLICITY
AS ONLY I KNEW HOW

IN AUGUST, I IMAGINED
AS FAR AS I COULD SEE

IN SEPTEMBER, I SLEPT AS
THE OCEAN AND SKY MET

IN OCTOBER, I WALTZED TO THE
RHYTHM OF COLORS IN MOTION

IN NOVEMBER, I THOUGHT TO
THANK MY LUCKY STARS,

IN DECEMBER, I WAS GIFTED
BEYOND MY PORTION.

EMD

A TYPICAL DAY ON A FARM

ARISING AT DAWN
WITH COWS TO MILK
CHICKENS TO FEED
AND CORN TO SILK

THE ROWS TO HOE
THE EGGS TO COUNT
THE BUTTER TO CHURN
THE HORSES TO MOUNT

THE GATES OPEN WIDE
FOR TRACTORS, SO BIG
GOATS TO FEED
MAYBE, EVEN A PIG

THE MELONS SO RIPE
THE YAMS AND POTATOES
THE PEAS, SO TENDER
AS ARE THE TOMATOES

HOPES FOR NO RAIN
AS ONE SMILES WITH CHARM
SO MUCH FOR A
TYPICAL DAY ON A FARM.

EMD

ON THE STREET WHERE I LIVED

ON THE STREET WHERE I LIVED,
THERE WERE SMALL FAMILIES, FAT
CHILDREN, SKINNY KIDS, MEAN PARENTS
GIRL FRIENDS, BOY FRIENDS, LARGE
HOUSES, SMALL HOMES, UNFENCED YARDS
GATED LAWNS, FLAT ROOFED HOUSES
STEPLED CHURCHES, NEON SIGNED
STORES, BRIGHTLY LIT, CAFES, YELLOW
HOUSES, GRAY HOMES, BRICK HOUSES
WHITE HOMES, NEW AUTOS, RAGGEDY
CARS, GREY-HAIRED OLD LADIES, LONG
HAIRED OLD MEN, IMPROPER KIDS, PRO-
PER CHILDREN, HOUSEWIVES, HOMEMAKERS
GARBAGE COLLECTORS, MECHANICS,
NURSES, MAIDS, PORTERS, CAB DRIVERS
ARMY MEN, NAVY MEN, SCHOOL TEACHERS
STUDENTS, COOKS, MORTICIANS, GARD-
NERS, CARPENTERS, AND ELECTRICIANS,
RAINY DAYS WITH CRAWFISH, SUNNY DAYS
WITH BUTTERFLIES, ROSE BUSHES, CAT-
TAILS AND CLOVERS, ALL
ON THE STREET WHERE I LIVED.

EMD

INSIDE ME

I FOUND NEWNESS OF SPRING
BLOSSOMS OF SUMMER
COLORS OF FALL
SLUMBER OF WITNTER.

EMD

WHAT IF

WHAT IF BIRDS COULDN'T SING
WHAT IF SNOWFLAKES DIDN'T FALL
WHAT IF STARS COULDN'T SHINE
WHAT IF REDWOODS WEREN'T SO TALL
WHAT IF FATHERS WEREN'T SO HANDY
WHAT IF DAUGHTERS WEREN'T SO SWEET
WHAT IF MOTHERS WEREN'T SO DEAR
WHAT IF SONS HAD TO STAY NEAT
WHAT IF DIAMONDS WEREN'T SO RARE
WHAT IF EMERALDS WEREN'T SO GREEN
WHAT IF SNOWMEN DIDN'T MELT
WHAT IF SANTA CLAUS WAS NEVER SEEN
WHAT IF FAIRIES WEREN'T SO GOOD
WHAT IF GLADIATORS DIDN'T WAR
WHAT IF ALASKA WASN'T SO COLD
WHAT IF COMETS DIDN'T FALL SO FAR
WHAT IF THE MEDITERRENEAN WASN'T SO BLUE
WHAT IF GAMES WEREN'T SO MUCH FUN
WHAT IF THE BUNNY NEVER HOPPED
WHAT IF RACES WERE NEVER RUN
WHAT IF THE ROSE DIDN'T HAVE THORNS
WHAT IF NIGHT DIDN'T FOLLOW DAY
WHAT IF ORVILLE AND WILBUR NEVER FLEW
WHAT IF JUNE DIDN'T FOLLOW MAY
WHAT IF GOLIATH WASN'T SO BIG
WHAT IF DAVID WASN'T SO SMALL
WHAT IF ROMEO DIDN'T KNOW JULIET
WHAT IF GOD DIDN'T LOVE US, ALL?

EMD

SNOWMAN

A SNOWMAN IS A MAN-SHAPED FIGURE MADE FROM SNOW. SINCE SNOWMEN ARE SHAPED AND FORMED ONLY IN COLD SNOWY WEATHER AND USUALLY AROUND THE ONCE-A-YEAR, CHRISTMAS SEASON, WE CAN APPRECIATE THE VERY TEMPORARY AND SHORT-LIVED APPEARANCE OF THE MAN-SHAPED SNOW ICE FIGURE.

ONE WILL FIND IT HARD TO THINK OF SNOWMEN WITHOUT THINKING OF SANTA CLAUS, REINDEER AND CHRISTMAS TREES. TO SOME, THE SNOWMAN IS SYMBOLIC ONLY, AND TO OTHERS, HE IS AS REAL AS THE CHRISTMAS TREE OR THE THANKSGIVING TURKEY.

WHAT ON EARTH WOULD WE DO WITHOUT SNOWMEN?

SANTA CLAUS

SANTA CLAUS IS A BRIGHTLY CLAD AND DISGUISED PERSON, BEARING GIFTS AT CHRISTMAS TIME. THERE ARE OTHER NAMES FOR THE GOOD TIDINGS OLD FELLOW, SUCH AS CHRIS KRINGLE AND SAINT NICHOLAS.

THE JOB OF THE TRADITIONAL GUY IS TO PREPARE, IN ADVANCE, GIFTS AND TOYS AT HIS TOY FACTORY, LOCATED SOMEWHERE AROUND THE NORTH POLE, WITH THE HELP OF HIS WIFE, MRS. SANTA CLAUS AND HIS ELVES. YOUNG CHILDREN FIND IT EASY TO MAKE BELIEVE AT CHRISTMAS-GIVING TIME, THUS, MAKING IT EASIER FOR THEM TO REALLY BELIEVE LATER IN THEIR LIVES.

WHAT ON EARTH WOULD WE DO WITHOUT SANTA?

ALASKA

ALASKA IS A STATE WITHIN THE UNITED STATES OF AMERICA. ALONG WITH HAWAII, IT WAS ADMITTED TO, THE, THEN, UNITED FORTY-EIGHT STATES, MAKING THE CURRENT FIFTY STATES.

ALASKA WAS ADDED, A VERY, VERY COLD AREA OF THE NEW ADDITION TO THE UNION. HAWAII WAS ADDED A VERY TROPICAL AREA OF THE COUNTRY. FOR MANY YEARS, BEFORE THE ADDITION OF ALASKA AND HAWAII, THE UNITED STATES FLAG WAS ONE OF FORTY-EIGHT STARS AND THE, STILL, THIRTEEN STRIPES, REPRESENTING THE THIRTEEN ORIGINAL COLONIES.

THE TWO, ADDITIONAL STATES WERE ADDED TO THE FORTY-EIGHT CONTIGUOUS ONES AFTER AIRPLANE FLIGHTS HAVE BECOME EASY MODES OF TRAVEL.

WHAT ON EARTH WOULD WE DO WITHOUT OUR COLDERST STATE, ALASKA?

STARS

A STAR IS A CELESTIAL BODY, VISIBLE AS LIGHT. A STAR HAS AN INDIVIDUALITY ALL ITS OWN, PRETTY MUCH LIKE A FLAKE OF SNOW. WHILE A SNOWFLAKE IS A VAPOR OF WATER, A STAR IS A UNIT OF LIGHT. THE BREVITY IN APPEARANCE AND DISAPPEARANCE IS SIMILAR IN, BOTH, STARS AND SNOWFLAKES.

(OVER)

(CON'D)

HUMAN BEINGS ARE A LOT LIKE STARS AND SNOWFLAKES IN THEIR INDIVIDUALITY IN DESIGN AND THEIR TEMPORARY EXISTENCE. THEY ARE, ALSO, ALIKE IN THAT THEY SHARE A BEAUTY THAT IS POSSIBLE, ONLY, BECAUSE THEY ARE TEMPORARY, LEADING US TO SAY THAT NOTHING GOOD LASTS FOREVER AND NOTHING PERMANENT IS BEAUTIFUL.

WHAT ON EARTH WOULD WE DO WITHOUT STARS?

REDWOODS

A REDWOOD IS A VERYTALL CONIFEROUS TIMBER TREE. THEY ARE SEEN, ALONG WITH THE OTHER STATELY TREES IN THE SEQUOIA AREA ESPECIALLY IN SOME PARTS OF NORTHERN CALIFORNIA. SOME OF THE TREE AREA IS PROTECTED AND USED FOR NATIONAL PARKS.

IT YEILDS A TYPE OF CONE, SIMILAR TO THE SMALLER PINE CONE, HENCE, THE REASON THEY ARE REFERRED TO AS CONIFERROUS.

REDWOODS ARE AMONG THE TALLEST AND OLDEST LIVING THINGS. MAKING EVEN THE TALLEST OF BEINGS SEEM DWARF IN COMPARISON.

NO WONDER IT IS SAID THAT ONLY GOD CAN MAKE A TREE.

WHAT ON EARTH WOULD WE DO WITHOUT THE REDWOODS?

WRIGHT BROTHERS

ORVILLE AND WILBUR WRIGHT WERE CREDITED WITH THE INVENTION OF THE AIRPLANE.

BEFORE ORVILLE AND WILBUR WRIGHT, ACT- UALLY, MADE THEIR IMPORTANT INVENTION FOR TRY-OUT AT KITTY HAWK, WE WERE COMFORTABLE TO JUST USE THE TRAINS, AUTOS AND SHIPS FOR TRANSPORTATION.

IF IT HAD NOT BEEN FOR THE WRIGHT BRO- THERS' INVENTION OF THE AIRPLANE, FOR SUCCESSFUL FLIGHT, IT WOULD, SURELY, HAVE BEEN SOMEONE ELSE, SOMEPLACE ELSE, FOR WE, OURSELVES, ARE NATURALLY CURIOUS ABOUT FLIGHT, AS EVIDENCED BY OUR AP- PENDAGES. SINCE WE DO NOT HAVE WINGS, THE AIRPLANE WOULD, SURELY HAVE A PLACE IN OUR LIVES.

WHAT ON EARTH WOULD WE DO WITHOUT AIR- PLANES?

GOLIATH

GOLIATH WAS A GIANT, WHO CHALLENGED A MUCH SMALLER PERSON, DAVID, TO A DUEL. NOT ALL GIANTS ARE BAD GUYS, SOME ARE JUST JOLLY. THE JOLLLY GREEN GIANT WAS NOT BAD, BUT, JUST JOLLY.

BIBLICAL SCRIPTURE TELLS OF GIANTS AFTER THE ORIGINAL CREATION IN THE BOOK OF GENESIS. WE CAN SUPPOSE THERE WERE MEN OF ALL SIZES, SINCE, THERE WERE MEN DOING ALL SORTS OF THINGS.

WHAT ON EARTH WOULD WE DO WITHOUT GOLIATH?

ROMEO AND JULIET

ROMEO AND JULIET WERE CHARACTERS IN A SHAKESPEARIAN WRITING THAT CAST THEM AS FATEFUL LOVERS.

ROMEO AND JULIET WERE TWO CHARACTERS IN WILLIAM SHAKESPEARE'S PLAYS. SHAKESPEARE IS WELL KNOWN FOR HIS SONNETS, PLAYS AND POETRY. LIKE MANY CHARACTERS IN HIS PLAYS, ROMEO AND JULIET WERE LOVERS, BUT, THE TWO MET WITH A VERY TRAGIC ENDING.

SOME OF SHAKESPEARES' OTHER WORKS, LIKE HAMLET, ARE, STILL, MUCH A PART OF THE THEATER, TODAY. SOME OTHER CHARACTERS IN SHAKESPEARE, TODAY, ARE JULIUS CAESAR AND OTHELLA

WHAT ON EARTH WOULD WE DO WITHOUT ROMEO AND JULIET?

GOD

GOD IS A DIEFIED SUPREME BEING OR SPIRIT. GOD IS SPIRIT, WHICH MEANS HE HAS ALWAYS BEEN PRESENT. HE IS, ALSO, LOVE, WHICH MEANS HE DOES NOT, JUST, SURVIVE OR EXIST, BUT, HE IS VITAL IN ORIGIN, CREATION AND PERPETUATION OF THE WORLD.

IT IS WRITTEN THAT NO MAN HAS SEEN THE FACE OF GOD. THIS IS BECAUSE MAN IS FLESH AND BLOOD AND SEES HIS LIKENESS, WHICH HE HAS PART IN ORIGINATING AND PERPETUATING.

(OVER)

(CON'D)

IT IS, ALSO, WRITTEN THAT THE HEAVENS DECLARE THE HANDIWORK OF GOD. THIS PUTS GOD VERY CLOSE AND NEAR IN ALL THAT WE ARE AND DO. GOD IS, BOTH, POWERFUL AND MIGHTY.

WHAT ON EARTH WOULD WE DO WITHOUT GOD?

ROSE

A ROSE IS A FLOWER OR BUD FROM A PRICKLY OR THORNY SHRUB OR BUSH. THE FLOWERS COME IN MANY COLORS AND ARE VERY LOVELY TO SMELL AND SEE. BOUQUETS OF ROSES, ESPECIALLY, LONG STEMMED ONES, FIND THEIR WAY INTO THE HEARTS AND MINDS OF MANY WOMEN ON OR AROUND VALENTINES AND MOTHER'S DAYS.

THE THORNS ARE ALMOST ALWAYS REMOVED FROM THE STEMS OF THE FLOWERS, BECAUSE THEY CAN CAUSE SERIOUS HARM IF LEFT ON THE FLOWERS OR BOUQUETS.

ROSEBUDS ARE AS BEAUTIFUL AS THE FULLY BLOSSOMED FLOWER. A ROSE IS SAID TO BE SO LOVELY BECAUSE IT IS SO SHORT-LIVED. IT PRESENTS ITS ALL AND, THEN, WITHERS TO NO MORE.

WHAT ON EARTH WOULD WE DO WITHOUT ROSES?

DAUGHTER

A DAUGHTER IS A FEMALE OFFSPRING. SHE IS KIND OF THE OPPOSITE OF THE SON. HER PLACE IN THE FAMILY IS EQUALLY IMPORTANT, IN THAT SHE, HERSELF, MAY GIVE BIRTH TO OFFSPRING ONE DAY OR TAKE THE NAME OF A NEW LINEAGE, THUS, ADDING NEW BRANCHES TO THE VERY IMPORTANT FAMILY TREE.

DAUGHTERS ARESAID TO BE "GIVEN" IN MARRIAGE BY THEIR FATHERS TO THEIR FUTURE HUSBAND, BECAUSE, UNTIL THEN, SHE SHARED THE NAME OF HER FATHER. A NEW SIR NAME WILL DIFINITELY GIVE HER NEW DIRECTION IN LIFE AND THIS IS VERY IMPORTANT TO MANY OTHERS, AFFECTED BY HER DECISION TO WED.

WHAT ON EARTH WOULD WE DO WITHOUT DAUGHTERS?

SON

A SON IS A MALE OFFSPRING OR THE MALE CHILD OF PARENTS. MALE CHILDREN MAY GROW UP TO BE FATHERS, UNCLES, BROTHERS, GRANDSONS AND NEPHEWS.

A SON IS VERY SPECIAL TO A FATHER AND MOTHER AND OCCUPIES A VERY IMPORTANT PLACE IN THE FAMILY. SONS CAN LOOK TO OTHER MALES FOR INFLUENCE AND GUIDANCE WHICH LETS THEM KNOW THAT THEIR PLACES AS SONS ARE VERY IMPORTANT TO OTHER MEMBERS OF THE FAMILY. A SON'S NAME, RECEIVED FROM HIS FATHER, PRESENTS A LINEAGE THAT IS VERY IMPORTANT TO THOSE BEFORE AND AFTER HIM IN THE FAMILY.

WHAT ON EARTH WOULD WE DO WITHOUT SONS?

MOTHER

A MOTHER IS A FEMALE PARENT. MOTHERS GIVE THE ACTUAL PHYSICAL BIRTH TO A CHILD AND NO ONE CAN DO THIS EXCEPT HER. THIS MAKES HER ROLE IN THE FAMILY A VERY IMPORTANT ONE AND NOT EASILY REPLACED.

MOTHERS PROVIDE A SENSE OF SECURITY IN MUCH THE SAME WAY FATHERS PROVIDE A SENSE OF STABILITY IN A FAMILY. BOTH ARE ESSENTIAL IN THE FAMILY UNIT. WHEN CIRCUMSTANCES HAPPEN THAT TAKES A MOTHER OR FEMALE PARENT FROM THE FAMILY, THINGS MAY NEVER BE QUITE THE SAME AGAIN. THE SECURITY SHE HELPS TO PROVIDE IS SOMETIMES IMPOSSIBLE TO ESTABLISH AGAIN.

WHAT ON EARTH WOULD WE DO WITHOUT MOTHERS?

FATHER

A FATHER IS A MALE PARENT. A FAMILY IS NOT POSSIBLE WITHOUT THE MALE PARENT, EVEN IF SITUATIONS FORCE HIM TO BE ABSENT FROM THE HOUSEHOLD. HIS PLACE IN THE FAMILY IS A PERMANENT ONE. FAMILIES ARE IMPORTANT AND FATHERS ARE VERY IMPORTANT AND INDESPENSABLE PERSONS IN THE LIVES OF FAMILY MEMBERS, ESPECIALLY, CHILDREN.

FATHERS PRESENT A STABILITY THAT IS VERY NESCESSARY IN THE FAMILY. HE IS A GUIDING INFLUENCE SINCE SIR NAMES ARE NESCESSARY FOR LEGAL IDENTITY.

WHAT ON EARTH WOULD WE DO WITHOUT FATHERS?

EMERALD

AN EMERALD IS A BRIGHT GREEN GEM. FOR THOSE WHOSE BIRTHSTONE IS EMERALD OR THOSE WHO FAVOR GREEN AS THE COLOR FOR GEMS, THE EMERALD IS VERY BEAUTIFUL. FOR OTHERS, IT MAY APPEAL ONLY AS A REMINDER THAT THE MONTH OF MAY IS IMPORTANT.

WHILE EMERALDS, LIKE TOPAZES, SAPPHIRES, AND RUBIES, MAY NOT EVER BE COVETED THE WAY THE DIAMOND IS SOUGHT, THE GEM IS BRIGHT AND PRETTY AND SURELY PRESENTS A PICTURE OF SIMPLE ELEGANCE AMONG THE MYRIAD OF OTHER MINERALS AND STONES. WHILE IT IS NOT A DIAMOND, IT IS STILL LOVED FOR ITS COLOR AND BRILLIANCE.

WHAT ON EARTH WOULD WE DO WITHOUT EMERALDS?

FAIRIES

A FAIRY (GOOD FAIRY), IS A SMALL IMAGINARY BEING, A MAKE-BELIEVE FRIEND OF SMALL CHILDREN, WHO TEND, TO BE ABLE TO WELCOME SUCH INTO THEIR LIVES. BELIEF IN SUCH HELPS THEM TO RELATE, AS INDIVIDUALS, IN THEIR WORLD, WHICH THEY MAY NOT BE ABLE IN THE REAL ADULT WORLD.

THE FARIES ARE REFERRED TO AS GOOD OR BAD, DEPENDING ON THE IMPRESSION THEY MAKE ON THE CHILD TROUGH THE CHILDS' IMAGINATION. NORMALLY, CHILDREN OUTGROW THIS PERIOD WITHOUT ANY ILL EFFECTS AND SOMETIMES ARE THE BETTER FOR HAVING HAD THE EXPERIENCE.

WHAT ON EARTH WOULD WE DO WITHOUT GOOD FAIRIES?

GLADIATOR

A GLADIATOR IS A WARRIER OR FIGHTER, LIKENED TO THE FIGHTER ENTERTAINERS OF THAT AGE IN HISTORY. THE GLADIATORS WOULD DUEL TO THE DEATH WITHOUT STOPPING TO ASK WHY. THE DUEL OR WARS WERE FOR THE ENTERTAINMENT OF RULERS OR ROYALTY.

MOVIES USED TO BE MADE OFTEN OF WARRING GLADIATORS, USING PARTICULAR TYPE OF ACTOR, SUCH AS CHARLESTON HESTON OR VICTOR MATURE OR RICHARD BURTON. THAT TYPE OF ACTING AND ACTORS ARE OUTDATED AND SELDOM USED ANYMORE. ADVANCES IN WESTERN CIVILIZATION AND CULTURE DID A LOT TO MAKE SUCH BABBARIC ACTIVITY OBSOLETE.

WHAT ON EARTH WOULD WE DO WITHOUT GLADIATORS?

BUNNY

A BUNNY IS ANOTHER WORD FOR A RABBIT OR EASTER BUNNY. JUST AS CHRISTMAS HAS ITS SECULAR INTEREST AS WELL AS ITS SPIRITUAL OR RELIGIOUS INTEREST AS THE BIRTHDAY OF CHRIST, EASTER, EVEN THOUGH A MEMORIAL OF JESUS CHRISTS' DEATH, HAS ITS SECULAR INTERESTS, ALSO.

THIS ONCE A YEAR REMEMBRANCE OF THE EASTER BUNNY, WHILE HIGHLY COMMERCIAL LIKE CHRISTMAS, IS APPRECIATED BY DRESSING UP IN SUNDAY ATTIRE AND ENJOYING, BOTH A SOLEMN AND JOYOUS OCASSION.

WHAT ON EARTH WOULD WE DO WITHOUT THE BUNNY?

GAMES

A GAME IS AN ACTIVITY OF FUN, PLAY OR FROLIC. THERE ARE BOARD GAMES, SUCH AS CHESS, MONOPOLY, BINGO AND SCRA-BBLE.

THERE ARE, ALSO, COURT GAMES, SUCH AS, TENNIS, BADMINTON AND BASKETBALL. THEN THERE ARE OUTSIDE GAMES PLAYED ON FIELDS OR DIAMONDS, SUCH AS TRACK, FOOTBALL AND BASEBALL. THERE ARE GAMES OF SPORT SUCH AS HUNTING, FISHING, SWIMMING RACING AND OLYMPIC-TYPE GAMES. SOME PEOPLE EVEN REFER TO LIFE AS THE "GAME OF LIFE" AT SOME POINT.

WHAT ON EARTH WOULD WE DO WITHOUT GAMES?

BIRDS

A BIRD IS A WARM-BLOODED EGG-LAYING FOUL. BIRDS, LIKE FISH HAVE APPENDAGES. BIRDS WINGS RESEMBLE OUR OUTSTRETCHED ARMS AND A FISH'S FINS. THE FLAP AND THE FLUTTER IS SIMILAR IN HUMANS, BIRDS AND FISH. EVEN WHEN THE APPENDAGES ARE NOT USED FOR FLAPPING TO FLY, OR FLUTTERING TO SWIM, THEY ARE IN PLACE FOR BALANCE.

LAND BIRDS, SUCH AS CHICKENS, GEESE AND DUCKS, OFFER A CONNECTION BETWEEN HUMANS AND BIRDS OF THE AIR AND FISH OF THE SEA.

WHAT ON EARTH WOULD WE DO WITHOUT BIRDS?

SNOWFLAKES

A SNOWFLAKE IS A CRYSTAL OF WATER VAPOR, SHAPED LIKE A FLAKE.

THE BEAUTY OF A SNOWFLAKE LIES IN ITS VAPOR EXISTENCE, TEMPORARY APPEARANCE AND ITS HERE FOR A MOMENT, THEN, GONE PRESENCE. LIKE STARS, NO TWO SNOWFLAKES ARE IDENTICAL IN SHAPE. LIKE EACH HUMAN PERSON IS DIFFERENT, EACH SNOWFLAKE HAS ITS OWN INDIVIDUAL DESIGN, BUT, UNLIKE HUMANS, THEIR TEMPORARY EXISTENCE PRESENTS A BEAUTY THAT IS REMEMBERED FOR A LONG TIME AFTER ITS PRESENCE IS GONE.

IN THE WORLD OF SNOWFLAKES, WE ARE SURE THAT EACH ONE HAS A NAME OR NUMBER OF IMPORTANCE ASSOCIATED, WITH ITS BEAUTY AND INDIVIDUALITY.

WHAT ON EARTH WOULD WE DO WITHOUT SNOWFLAKES?

DIAMOND

A DIAMOND IS A ROCK-HARD, BRILLIANT MINERAL, THAT CONSISTS OF CRYSTALLINE CARBON. THE GEM IS NOT THE RAREST, BUT, BECAUSE OF ITS CLARITY AND BRILLIANCE IT IS HIGHLY RATED FOR ITS BEAUTY AND SIMPLICITY.

A DIAMOND IS SO HARD THAT IT MAY ACTUALLY CUT INTO OTHER STONES OR GEMS, ESPECIALLY, GLASS. A DIAMOND IS, ALSO, COVETED FOR ITS TYPE OF METAMORPHIC CHANGE FROM SOMETHING UGLY TO SOMETHING VERY LOVELY WITH NOTHING ADDED TO THE VIRGINITY OF THE MINERAL. LIKE GOLD, IT PROUDLY SAYS LOOK WHAT A LITTLE POLISH WILL DO TO BRING ABOUT A SHINE.

WHAT ON EARTH WOULD WE DO WITHOUT A DIAMOND?

RACES

A RACE IS A CONTEST OF SPEED OR ENDURANCE. RACES ARE RUN FOR MANY DIFFERENT REASONS. SOME OF THE REASONS ARE FOR FAME, FUN, FORTUNE, SPORT AND SIMPLE EXERCISE ENJOYMENT.

A RACE MAY INVOLVE AS FEW AS TWO INDIVIDUALS OR WITH MANY PARTICIPANTS AS WITH OLYMPIC GAMES RACES, MARATHON RACES AND SIMPLIER TEAM RACES. THE SUMMER AND WINTER OLYMPIC GAMES RACES HELD EVERY FOUR YEARS IN DIFFERENT PARTS OF THE WORLD ARE VERY IMPORTANT EVENTS TO MILLIONS OF PEOPLE IN SEVERAL COUNTRIES ACROSS THE WORLD. THIS INTEREST HELPS TO SUPPORT PEACE AMONG THE COUNTRIES AND GOVERNMENTS INVOLVED.

WHAT ON EARTH WOULD WE DO WITHOUT RACES?

COMETS

A COMET IS A SMALL BRIGHT CELESTIAL BODY WITH A TAIL OF LIGHT ALLOWING IT TO SEEM AS THOUGH IT IS FALLING TOWARDS THE EARTH.

ONE OF THE MOST COMMON AND STUDIED COMETS IS HALEY'S COMET. IT GETS ITS NAME FROM THE CONSTELLATION FOR WHICH IT IS A PART. SOMETIMES STUDIES OF COMETS ARE POSSIBLE ON VERY CLEAR NIGHTS AND SKIES, BUT, NORMALLY, A TELESCOPE IS NESCESSARY TO EXAMINE THE SHAPE, MOVEMENT AND RELATION TO OTHER CELESTIAL BODIES.

WHAT ON EARTH WOULD WE DO WITHOUT COMETS?

JUNE

JUNE IS THE SIXTH MONTH OF THE YEAR. IT COMES BEFORE THE MONTH OF JULY AND JUST AFTER THE MONTH OF MAY. JUNE IS THE BEGINNING OF SUMMER MONTH, WHICH IS USUALLY AROUND THE TWENTY-FIRST DAY.

THE MONTH OF JUNE IS, ALSO, A FAVORITE MONTH FOR THOSE CONSIDERING NUPTIALS OR WEDDINGS. JUNE IS CONSIDERED A PRETTY NAME FOR A GIRL AS MANY GIRLS ARE CALLED JUNE AS A FIRST OR MIDDLE NAME.

THE BIRTHSTONE COLOR FOR THE MONTH OF JUNE IS A PRETTY PINK, MAKING IT A PRETTY MONTH FOR BRIDES. THE MONTH IS, ALSO, KNOWN AS A FAVORITE FOR GRADUATIONS OR COMMENCEMENT EXERCISES.

THE MONTH IS A COMFORTABLE MONTH, SINCE, IT IS MARKING THE MIDDLE OF THE CALENDAR IT IS A TIME OF THE YEAR TO THINK OF VACATIONS AND LEAVE OF ABSCENSES FOR RELAXING AND COMFORT.

WHAT ON EARTH WOULD WE DO WITHOUT THE MONTH OF JUNE?

NIGHT

NIGHT IS THE EVENING OR SECOND PART OF A DAY WITH THE MORNING BEING THE FIRST PART.

NIGHT IS SAID TO BE THE TIME WHEN IT IS BEST TO SLEEP OR DO NOTHING, WHENEVER POSSIBLE.

NIGHT SEEMS TO BRING OUT THE SPOOKY CREATURES OF HALLOWEEN SPIRIT. IT HOLDS A LOT OF SUPERSTITIOUS FABLES CONCERNING GHOSTS, WITCHES AND GOBLINS.

THE MOON IS THE LIGHT FOR THE NIGHT OR EVENING. THE MOON IS CONSIDERED THE LESSER LIGHT THAN THE SUN AS FAR AS THE CREATION STORY GOES. THE STARS ARE, ALSO, PROVIDERS OF LIGHT FOR THE NIGHT. A MOONLIT NIGHT CAN BE EVERY BIT AS BEAUTIFUL AS A SUNNY DAY.

THE NIGHT OF EIGHT TO TWELVE HOURS IS PREFERRED BY MANY WORKERS AND IS SOMETIMES CALLED THE GRAVEYARD SHIFT, BECAUSE OF THE SPOOKY TALES ASSOCIATED WITH SUPERSTITION AND MAKE-BELIEVE.

WHAT ON EARTH WOULD WE DO WITHOUT THE NIGHT?

DAVID

DAVID, THE SON OF JESSE, THE BETHLEMITE, WAS CUNNING IN PLAYING AND A MIGHTY VALIANT MAN AND A MAN OF WAR AND PRUDENT IN MATTERS AND A COMELY PERSON AND THE LORD IS WITH HIM, A FAVORITE OF KING SAUL. DAVID WAS THE 'GOPHER' OR ERRAND BOY FOR HIS THREE ELDER BROTHERS, WHO WENT TO WAR WITH THE PHILISTINES. THE GIANT, GOLIATH, WAS SLAIN BY DAVID WITH A SLINGSHOT AND STONE FROM A BROOK.

AND DAVID WENT ON AND GREW AND THE LORD, GOD OF HOSTS WAS WITH HIM. AND DAVID PERCEIVED THAT THE LORD HAD ESTABLISHED HIM KING OVER ISRAEL AND THAT HE HAD EXALTED HIS KINGDOM FOR HIS PEOPLE, ISRAEL'S SAKE. "AND NOW, O LORD, GOD, THOU ART THAT GOD AND THY WORDS BE TRUE AND THOU HAST PROMISED THIS GOODNESS UNTO THY SERVANT. THEREFORE, NOW LET I PLEASE THEE TO BLESS THE HOUSE OF THY SERVANT, THAT IT MAY CONTINUE FOREVER BEFORE THEE FOR THOU O LORD, GOD HAST SPOKEN IT AND WITH THY BLESSING LET THE HOUSE OF THY SERVANT BE BLESSED FOREVER".

WHAT ON EARTH WOULD WE DO WITHOUT DAVID?

MEDITERRANEAN

MEDITERRANEAN IS A SEA, LOCATED JUST NORTH OF LOWER EGYPT NEAR THE GAZA STRIP, NEAR CYPRUS AND SYRIA AND THE TIGRIS, EUPHRATES AND NILE RIVERS AND THE RED AND CASPIAN SEA, JUST BELOW ASIA MINOR.

THE CRESCENT SHAPED AREA LOCATED NEXT TO THE MEDITERRANEAN IS THE AREA THAT IS JORDAN, LEBANON, TURKEY AND SYRIA. THE ONCE, ESPECIALLY, FERTILE AREA LOCATED BETWEEN THE TIGRIS AND THE EUPHRATES RIVERS, PROCEEDING TOWARD THE PERSIAN GULF INCLUDES THE AREA THAT IS IRAQ, ONCE REFERRED TO AS MESOPOTAMIA OR "LAND BETWEEN THE RIVERS" IN GREEK. SOME OF THE WORLD'S FIRST CITIES ARE SAID TO HAVE HAD THEIR BEGINNING IN THIS AREA, ALONG WITH SOME OF THE EARLIEST CIVILIZATIONS AND CULTURES. SUCH A CIVILIZATION WAS THE SUMERIANS AROUND 3000 B.C. THE PHOENICIANS, AN EARLY PEOPLE OR CIVILIZATION WERE VERY POLYTHEISTIC AS WERE THE SUMERIANS. BUT, THE COMING OF THE HEBREWS BROUGHT THE IDEA OF ONE ALL-POWERFUL GOD OR "YAHWEH" AND WHAT, IS POPULAR TODAY, MONOTHEISM OF WHICH JUDAISM, CHRISTAINITY AND ISLAM ARE BASED.

WHAT ON EARTH WOULD WE DO WITHOUT THE MEDITERRANEAN?

"THE TIMES, IN FACT, ARE CHANGING,
DARLING"

SAME TIME NEXT YEAR

"A CANDLE BURNED AT BOTH ENDS WON'T
LAST THE NIGHT"

A RIVER RUNS THROUGH IT

"MENDACITY IS A SYSTEM WE LIVE IN"

CAT ON A HOT TIN ROOF

"FRANKLY, I DON'T GIVE A DAMN"

GONE WITH THE WIND

"I DON'T WANT TO STAY WITH YOU, MOMMY!"

CARRIE

SING UNTO THE LORD WITH THANKS-
GIVING.......PSALM 147:7

CHERISH THE LOVE

LET'S TAKE A WALK TOGETHER NEAR THE OCEAN SHORE, HAND IN HAND, YOU AND I, LET'S CHERISH EVERY MOMENT WE HAVE BEEN GIVEN, TIME IS PASSING BY.

I HOPE AND PRAY BEFORE I LAY DOWN BY YOUR SIDE, IF YOU RE-CEIVE YOUR CALLING BEFORE I AWAKE, COULD I MAKE IT THRU THE NIGHT?

CHERISH THE LOVE, WE HAVE, WE SHOULD CHERISH THE LIFE WE LIVE, CHERISH THE LOVE, CHERISH THE LIFE, CHERISH THE LOVE.

CHERISH THE LOVE WE HAVE, BOTH AS LONG AS WE BOTH, SHALL LIVE CHERISH THE LOVE, CHERISH THE LIFE, CHERISH THE LOVE.

THE WORLD IS ALWAYS CHANGING NOTHING STAYS THE SAME. BUT, LOVE WILL STAND THE TEST OF TIME, THE NEXT LIFE THAT WE LIVE IN RE-MAINS TO BE SEEN. WILL YOU BE BY MY SIDE? I HOPE AND PRAY. CHERISH THE LOVE, CHERISH THE LIFE.

KOOL AND THE GANG

BUY ME A ROSE (FOR R.L.H.)

HE WORKS HARD TO GIVE HER ALL HE THINKS SHE WANTS. BUT, IT TEARS HER APART CAUSE NOTHING'S FOR HER HEART. HE PULLS IN LATE, TO WAKE HER WITH A KISS GOOD NIGHT, IF HE COULD ONLY READ HER MIND, SHE'D SAY, BUY ME A ROSE, CALL ME FROM WORK, OPEN A DOOR FOR ME, WHAT WOULD IT HURT? SHOW ME YOU LOVE ME BY THE LOOK IN YOUR EYES. THESE ARE THE LITTLE THINGS I NEED THE MOST IN MY LIFE, NOW, THE DAYS HAVE GROWN TO YEARS OF FEELING ALL ALONE AS SHE SITS AND WONDERS IF ALL SHE IS DOING IS WRONG, CAUSE, LATELY, SHE'D TRY ANYTHING JUST TO TURN HIS HEAD. WOULD IT MAKE A DIFFERENCE IF SHE SAID, IF SHE SAID, BUY ME A ROSE? AND THE MORE THAT HE LIVES, THE LESS THAT HE TRIES TO SHOW HER THE LOVE THAT HE HOLDS INSIDE AND THE MORE THAT SHE GIVES, THE MORE THAT HE SEES THAT THIS IS THE STORY OF YOU AND ME. SO I BOUGHT YOU A ROSE ON THE WAY FROM WORK TO OPEN THE DOOR TO A HEART THAT I HURT, AND I HOPE YOU NOTICE THIS LOOK IN MY EYES, CAUSE I'M GONNA HOLD YOU TONIGHT AND DO ALL THOSE LITTLE THINGS FOR THE REST OF MY LIFE.

LUTHER VANDROSS

ONCE, WE WERE LOVERS

WE SHARED A LIFE
WE SHARED A HEART
BUT, WHAT WE UNITED
SEEMS TO BE BREAKING APART
IT'S A HAUNTING PAIN
GOES RIGHT TO THE CORE
NOW, WE'RE DIVIDING
WHATS MINE FROM WHATS YOURS,
I'LL KEEP THE SAME OLD THINGS
I HAD WHEN WE MET
AND YOU'LL KEEP WHAT'S YOURS
CAUSE THAT WOULD ONLY BE FAIR
BUT, WHAT ABOUT THE HEART
WE, BOTH, CREATED TOGETHER?
WE USED TO BE THE TOAST OF THE TOWN
WE USED TO HAVE THE BEST LOVE OF ALL
WE HAD BLUE SKIES, BUT,
THEY CAME FALLING DOWN
WHAT HAPPENED TO US?
YOU AND I, ONCE, WERE LOVERS.
NO CHEATING HEARTS AND
NO ONE DID WRONG,
SO WHY DID WE BREAK,
CAN'T SAY OUR LOVE WASN'T STRONG
BUT, I KNOW WITH TIME
THAT THINGS START TO MEND.
SO, LETS FIX THESE HEARTS SO,
THEY CAN'T BE BROKEN AGAIN,
YOU NEED A MAN, WHO,
SEES HOW LONELY YOU'VE BEEN
DON'T WORRY, I'LL START
ALL OVER AND THEN
WE'LL GET BACK THE HEART
THAT WE, BOTH, CREATED TOGETHER

(OVER)

(CON'D)

LAST NIGHT I CRIED, BUT,
GIRL, YOU WERE NOT HERE,
SO, IT WAS JUST A
BIG WASTE OF TEARS.
BUT, THEN, I SMILED, I HEARD
YOUR VOICE IN MY EAR, TELLING ME
YOU WISH IT COULD BE LIKE
IT WAS IN THE BEGINNING.

LUTHER VANDROSS

YOU LIGHT UP MY LIFE

SO MANY NIGHTS, I'D SIT BY MY WINDOW
WAITING FOR SOMEONE TO SEND ME HER SONG
SO MANY DREAMS, I KEPT DEEP INSIDE ME
ALONE IN THE DARK, BUT, NOW,
YOU'VE COME ALONG AND YOU LIGHT UP MY
LIFE, YOU GIVE ME HOPE TO CARRY ON,
YOU LIGHT UP MY DAYS AND FILL MY NIGHTS
WITH SONG.

ROLLING AT SEA ADRIFT ON THE WATERS,
COULD IT BE, FINALLY, I'M TURNING FOR
HOME, FINALLY, A CHANCE TO SAY, HEY,
I LOVE YOU. NEVER, AGAIN, TO BE ALL
ALONE. YOU LIGHT UP MY LIFE, YOU GIVE ME
HOPE TO CARRY ON, YOU LIGHT UP MY DAYS
AND FILL MY NIGHTS WITH SONG, YOU LIGHT
UP MY LIFE, YOU GIVE ME HOPE TO CARRY
ON, YOU LIGHT UP MY DAYS AND FILL MY
NIGHTS WITH SONG.

AND IT CAN'T BE WRONG, WHEN IT FEELS
SO RIGHT, BECAUSE YOU LIGHT UP MY LIFE.

KENNY ROGERS

THEY SAID YOU NEEDED ME (FOR C.W.)
GOODBY, SO LONG
WERE THE LAST WORDS FROM YOU
SEEMS LIKE YOU'RE OVER
ALL THE GOODNESS, WE KNEW
YOU THINK THAT YOU DON'T
YOU DON'T NEED NO ONE
WELL, I WAS TALKING TO SOME OF YOUR
FRIENDS JUST TO SEE HOW EVERYONE
WAS DOING AND THEY SAID YOU NEEDED
ME, SAID IT WAS SOMETHING YOU'D
NEVER ADMIT, BUT, IT WAS HARD TO SEE
YOU GOING THROUGH IT. THEY SAID YOU
NEEDED ME. GUESS I'LL SUFFER TIL
I'M WHERE I BELONG
I'M UNDER THE PRESSURE
BUT, I'LL KEEP BEING STRONG
YOU SAY T HAT YOU'RE STRONG
YOU SAY THAT YOU DON'T NEED ANYONE
WHAT IN THE WORLD ARE YOU
TELLING YOUR FRIENDS?
THEY SAID YOU NEEDED ME
I KNOW THAT PEOPLE TALK
JUST FOR THE THRILL
BUT, THE FACT OF THE MATTER IS STILL
THEY SAID YOU NEEDED ME.
TAKE YOUR TIME, REINVENT YOUR MIND
YOU'LL FEEL BETTER, YOU'LL FEEL
STRONGER. THEN DECIDE IF I'M
IN YOUR LIFE FOREVER OR LONGER
YOU THINK THAT YOU'RE STRONG
YOU THINK THAT YOU DON'T, YOU DON'T
NEED NO ONE. WELL, I WAS TALKING TO
SOME OF YOUR FRIENDS, JUST TO SEE HOW
EVERYONE WAS DOING AND THEY SAID YOU
NEEDED ME, SAID IT WAS SOMETHING YOU'D
NEVER ADMIT, BUT, IT WAS HARD TO SEE
YOU GOING THROUGH IT. THEY SAID YOU
NEEDED ME. LUTHER VANDROSS

THAT'S WHAT LOVE IS FOR

SOMETIMES WE MAKE IT HARDER THAN
IT IS. WE TAKE A PERFECT NIGHT AND
FILL IT WITH WORDS WE DON'T MEAN
DARK SIDE'S BEST UNSEEN, AND WE
WONDER WHY WE FEEL THIS WAY.

SOMETIMES I WONDER IF WE REALLY FEEL
THE SAME, WHY WE CAN BE SO UNKIND,
QUESTIONING THE STRONGEST OF HEARTS,
THAT'S WHEN WE MUST START, BELIEVING
IN THE ONE THING THAT'S GOTTEN US
THIS FAR.

THAT'S WHAT LOVE IF FOR, TO HELP US
THRU IT, THAT'S WHAT LOVE IS FOR,
NOTHING ELSE CAN DO IT, MELT OUR
DEFENSES, BRING US BACK TO OUR SENSES,
GIVE US STRENGTH TO TRY ONCE MORE,
BABY THAT'S WHAT LOVE IS FOR.

SOMETIMES I SEE YOU AND YOU DON'T
KNOW I AM THERE AND I'M WASHED AWAY
BY EMOTIONS, I HOLD DEEP DOWN INSIDE,
GETTING STRONGER WITH TIME. IT'S
LIVING THRU THE FIRE AND HOLDING ON
WITH FINE. THAT'S WHAT LOVE IS FOR.
TO ROUND OUT THE EDGES, DROP US DOWN
FROM THE LEDGES, GIVE US STRENGTH TO
TRY ONCE MORE, BABY, THAT'S WHAT LOVE
IS FOR, BELIEVING IN THE ONE THING
THAT'S GOTTEN US THIS FAR, THAT'S
WHAT LOVE IS FOR.

AMY GRANT

HELLO

I HAVE BEEN ALONE, WITH YOU INSIDE
MY MIND, AND IN MY DREAMS, I HAVE
KISSED YOUR LIPS A THOUSAND TIMES.
I, SOMETIMES SEE YOU PASS OUTSIDE
MY DOOR, HELLO, IS IT ME YOU'RE
LOOKING FOR? I CAN SEE IT IN YOUR
EYES, I CAN SEE IT IN YOUR SMILE
YOU'RE ALL I HAVE EVER WANTED AND MY
ARMS ARE OPEN WIDE, CAUSE, YOU KNOW
JUST WHAT TO SAY AND YOU KNOW JUST
WHAT TO DO AND I WANT TO TELL YOU
SO MUCH, I LOVE YOU.

I LONG TO SEE THE SUNLIGHT IN YOUR
HAIR, AND TELL YOU, TIME AND TIME
AGAIN HOW MUCH I CARE. SOMETIMES,
I FEEL MY HEART WILL OVERFLOW.
HELLO, I'VE JUST GOT TO LET YOU
KNOW, CAUSE I WONDER WHERE YOU ARE
AND I WONDER WHAT YOU DO. ARE YOU
SOMEWHERE, FEELING LONELY OR IS
SOMEONE LOVING YOU? TELL ME HOW TO
WIN YOUR HEART, FOR I HAVEN'T GOT
A CLUE, BUT, LET ME START BY TELL-
ING, I LOVE YOU.

LIONEL RICHIE

SING UNTO THE LORD, WITH THANKS-
GIVING....PSALM 147:7

REFUGE (WHEN IT'S COLD OUTSIDE)
I PRAYED FOR BETTER DAYS TO COME
PRAYED THAT I WOULD SEE THE SUN
CAUSE LIFE IS SO BURDENSOME
WHEN EVERY DAY'S A RAINY ONE.
BUT, SUDDENLY THERE'S NO MORE CLOUDS
AND I BELIEVE, WITHOUT A DOUBT
THAT HEAVEN SENT AN ANGEL DOWN
YOU KNOW AND I KNOW
FRIENDS COME AND FRIENDS GO
STORMS RISE AND WINDS BLOW
BUT, ONE THING I KNOW FOR SURE
WHEN IT'S COLD OUTSIDE
THERE'S NO NEED TO WORRY CAUSE I'M
SO WARM INSIDE, CAUSE WE'RE IN LOVE
I KNOW IT'LL BE ALRIGHT, NOW, PEACE
IS SO HARD TO FIND. WE ARE
TERRORIZED AND VICTIMIZED, BUT,
THAT'S WHEN I CLOSE MY EYES AND
THINK OF YOU TO EASE MY MIND.
YOU TAKE ME TO ANOTHER PLACE
WHERE THERE'S NO MORE WAR,
JUST LOVE AND GRACE. BABY, YOU
RESTORE MY FAITH, I KNOW THIS
STRUGGLE'S NOT IN VAIN
YOU KNOW AND I KNOW THROUGH ALL
THE BATTLES, BAGHDAD TO ISRAEL
ONE THING I KNOW FOR SURE,
WE'RE IN LOVE, I KNOW IT'LL
BE ALRIGHT.

JOHN LEGEND

EVERGREEN

LOVE, SOFT AS AN EASY CHAIR
LOVE, FRESH AS THE MORNING AIR
ONE LOVE, THAT IS SHARED BY TWO
I HAVE FOUND WITH YOU.

LIKE A ROSE
UNDER THE APRIL SNOW
I WAS ALWAYS CERTAIN
LOVE WOULD GROW
LOVE, AGELESS AND EVERGREEN

SELDOM SEEN BY TWO
YOU AND I WILL MAKE EACH
NIGHT A FIRST AND EVERY DAY
A BEGINNING

SPIRITS RISE AND THEIR DANCE
IS UNREHEARSED
WARM AND EXCITED
BECAUSE WE HAVE THE
BRIGHTEST LOVE

TWO LIGHTS, TWO LIGHTS THAT SHINE
AS ONE, MORNING GLORY AND
MIDNIGHT SUN
TIME WILL CHANGE THE MEANING OF
ONE LOVE, AGELESS AND EVER, EVERGREEN.

KENNY ROGERS

SAVED THE BEST FOR LAST

SOMETIMES THE SNOW COMES DOWN IN JUNE, SOMETIMES THE SUN GOES AROUND THE MOON, I SEE THE PASSION IN YOUR EYES, SOMETIMES IT'S ALL A BIG SURPRISE, CAUSE THERE WAS A TIME WHEN ALL I DID WAS WISH YOU'D TELL ME THIS IS LOVE, IT'S NOT THE WAY I HOPED OR HOW I PLANNED.

BUT, SOMEHOW IT'S ENOUGH, AND NOW WE'RE STANDING FACE TO FACE, ISN'T THIS WORLD A CRAZY PLACE? JUST WHEN I THOUGHT OUR CHANCE HAD PASSED,YOU GO AND SAVE THE BEST FOR LAST.

ALL OF THE NITES, YOU CAME TO ME WHEN SOME SILLY GIRL HAD SET YOU FREE, YOU WONDERED HOW YOU'D MAKE IT THRU. I WONDERED WHAT WAS WRONG WITH YOU, CAUSE HOW COULD YOU GIVE YOUR LOVE TO SOMEONE ELSE AND SHARE YOUR DREAMS WITH ME? SOMETIMES THE VERY THING YOU'RE LOOKING FOR IS THE ONE THING YOU CAN'T SEE, BUT, NOW WE'RE STANDING FACE TO FACE, ISN'T THIS WORLD A CRAZY PLACE?

VANESSA WILLIAMS

STRUGGLES AND TRIBULATIONS ARE VERY MUCH A PART OF EVERYONE'S LIFE. SOMETIMES IT IS A MATTER OF PROBLEMS AND SUFFERINGS WHICH CAN SURELY TEST OUR MENTAL AND PHYSICAL RESISTANCE AND PERHAPS, EVEN SHAKE OUR FAITH. BUT, EXPERIENCE TEACHES THAT DAILY DIFFICULTIES BY GOD'S GRACE, OFTEN CONTRIBUTE TO PEOPLE'S GROWTH AND CHARACTER.

POPE JOHN PAUL II

YOUR SONG

IT'S A LITTLE BIT FUNNY,
THIS FEELING INSIDE
I AM NOT ONE OF THOSE
WHO CAN EASILY HIDE
I DON'T HAVE MUCH MONEY
BUT, IF I DID, I'D BUY A BIG HOUSE
WHERE WE BOTH COULD LIVE.

IF I WAS A SCULPTER, BUT THEN AGAIN,
NO, OR A MAN WHO MAKES POTIONS IN
THE TRAVELING SHOW. I KNOW IT'S
NOT MUCH, BUT, IT'S THE BEST I CAN DO,
MY GIFT IS MY SONG AND THIS ONE'S FOR
YOU, AND YOU CAN TELL EVERYBODY THAT
THIS IS YOUR SONG, IT MAY BE QUITE
SIMPLE, BUT, NOW THAT IT'S DONE, I
HOPE YOU DON'T MIND THAT I PUT DOWN
THE WORDS, HOW WONDERFUL LIFE IS
WHILE YOU'RE IN THE WORLD.

I SAT ON THE ROOF, KICKED OFF THE MOSS
WERE A FEW OF THE VERSES, WELL, THEY
HAVE GOT ME QUITE CROSS, BUT, THE SUN'S
BEEN QUITE KIND, WHILE I WROTE THIS
SONG, IT'S FOR PEOPLE LIKE YOU THAT
KEEP IT TURNED ON. SO EXCUSE ME FOR
FORGETTING, BUT, THESE THINGS, I DO,
YOU SEE I'VE FORGOTTEN IF THEY ARE
GREEN OR BLUE. ANYWAY, THE THING IS,
WHAT I REALLY NEED, THESE ARE THE
SWEETEST SKIES, I'VE EVER SEEN.

ELTON JOHN

LIFT EVERY VOICE AND SING

LIFT EVERY VOICE AND SING
TIL EARTH AND HEAVEN RING
RING WITH THE HARMONYS OF LIBERTY.

LET OUR REJOICING RISE HIGH AS THE
LISTENING SKIES, LET IT RESOUND LOUD
AS THE ROLLING SEA.

SING A SONG, FULL OF THE FAITH THAT
THE DARK PAST HAST HAS TAUGHT US, SING
A SONG, FULL OF THE HOPE THAT THE
PRESENT HAS BROUGHT US.

FACING THE RISING SUN OF A NEW DAY
BEGUN. LET US MARCH ON TIL VICTORY
IS WON.

GOD OF OUR WEARY YEARS
GOD OF OUR SILENT TEARS
THOU, WHO HAST BROUGHT US, THUS FAR
ON THE WAY. THOU, WHO HAST, BY THY
MIGHT, LED US INTO THE LIGHT, KEEP
US FOREVER IN THE PATH, WE PRAY

LEST OUR FEET STRAY FROM THE PLACES
OF GOD, WHERE WE MADE THEE. LEST
OUR HEARTS, DRUNK WITH THE WINE OF
THE WORLD, WE FORGET THEE.
SHADOWED BENEATH THY NAME, MAY WE,
FOREVER STAND, TRUE TO OUR GOD, TRUE
TO OUR NATIVE LAND.

(50 GREAT SONGS)

GOD BLESS AMERICA

GOD BLESS AMERICA
LAND THAT I LOVE
STAND BESIDE US
AND GUIDE US,
THROUGH THE NIGHT, WITH THY
LIGHT FROM ABOVE,
FROM THE MOUNTAIN, TO THE PRARIE
TO THE OCEAN, WHITE WITH FOG
GOD BLESS AMERICA
MY HOME, SWEET HOME,
GOD BLESS AMERICA
MY HOME, SWEET HOME.

PLEDGE OF ALLEGIANCE

I PLEDGE ALLEGIANCE TO THE FLAG
OF THE UNITED STATES OF AMERICA
AND TO THE REPUBLIC, FOR WHICH
IT STANDS, ONE NATION, UNDER GOD,
INDIVISIBLE, WITH LIBERTY AND
JUSTICE FOR ALL.

GOD LEADS US ALONG

SOME THROUGH THE WATERS,
SOME THROUGH THE FLOOD
SOME THROUGH THE FIRE, BUT,
ALL THROUGH THE BLOOD
SOME, THROUGH GREAT SORROW
BUT, GOD GIVES A SONG
IN THE NIGHT SEASON AND
AND ALL THE DAY LONG.

YOUNG

LEO
YOU MAY BE KING OR A LOVER OR A COWARDLY LION'S, BUT, YOU MUST LIKE THE MONTHS OF JULY AND AUGUST.

VIRGO
YOU MAY LOOK AT THINGS AS THOUGH THEY WERE GREEK, BUT, YOU DO ENJOY THE MONTHS OF AUGUST AND SEPTEMBER.

LIBRA
YOU LOVE HARMONY AND BALANCE AND FIND IT EASY TO LIKE THE MONTHS OF SEPTEMBER AND OCTOBER.

SCORPIO
YOU MAY NOT FIND CRUSTY THINGS APPEALING, BUT, YOU DO ENJOY THE MONTHS OF OCTOBER AND NOVEMBER.

SAGITARUS
YOU, TOO, MAY FIND DESTINY IN THE STARS BUT, YOU WILL LOVE THE MONTHS OF NOVEMBER AND DECEMBER.

CANCER
YOUR FAVORITES MAY NOT BE CRUSTACEANS AT ALL, BUT, YOU WILL LOVE THE MONTHS OF JUNE AND JULY.

CAPRICORN
YOU MAY FREFER CORN TO MAIZE, BUT, YOU MUST FEEL AT HOME WITH THE MONTHS OF DECEMBER AND JANUARY.

AQUAARIUS
YOU MAY NOT BELIEVE IN MAGIC AND GENIES IN BOTTLES, BUT, YOU MUST LOVE THE MONTHS OF JANUARY AND FEBRUARY.

PISCES
YOU MAY NOT EAT FISH OR CAN'T WAIT UNTIL FRIDAY COMES, BUT, YOU MUST FEEL GOOD ABOUT THE MONTHS OF FEB-RUARY AND MARCH.

ARIES
YOU MAY GET FUNNY LITTLE FEELINGS ABOUT CREEPY, CRAWLING LITTLE THINGS, BUT, YOU MUST ENJOY THE MONTHS OF MARCH AND APRIL.

TARUS
YOU DON'T HAVE TO BE BULLISH, BUT, YOU DO HAVE TO ENJOY THE MONTHS OF APRIL AND MAY.

GEMINI
YOUR WORLD MAY FEEL TOPSY TURVY MOST OF THE TIME, BUT, YOU MUST LIKE THE MONTHS OF MAY AND JUNE.

AMERICA THE BEAUTIFUL

O BEAUTIFUL, FOR SPACIOUS SKIES
FOR AMBER WAVES OF GRAIN
FOR PURPLE MOUNTAINS, MAJESTIES
ABOVE THE FRUITED PLAIN
AMERICA, AMERICA
GOD SHED HIS GRACE ON THEE
AND CROWNED THY GOOD WITH BROTHERHOOD
FROM SEA TO SHINING SEA

O BEAUTIFUL FOR PATRIOT DREAM
THAT SEES BEYOND THE REARS
THINE ALABASTER CITIES, GLEAM
UNDIMMED BY HUMAN TEARS
AMERICA, AMERICA
GOD SHED HIS GRACE ON THEE

KATHERINE LEE BATES

STAR SPANGLED BANNER

O SAY CAN YOU SEE
BY THE DAWN'S EARLY LIGHT
WHAT SO PROUDLY, WE HAILED
BY THE TWILIGHT'S LAST GLEAMING
AND THE ROCKETS RED GLARE, THE
BOMBS, BURSTING IN AIR, GAVE PROOF
THAT OUR FLAG WAS STILL THERE,
O SAY DOES THAT STAR-SPANGLES
BANNER, YET, WAVE, OVER THE LAND
OF THE FREE AND THE HOME OF BRAVE.
FRANCIS SCOTT KEY

GOD MOVES IN MYSTERIOUS WAYS
HIS WONDERS TO PERFORM
HE PLANTS HIS FOOTSTEPS IN THE SEA
AND RULES UPON THE STORM.

COWPER

THE FRAGRANCE OF GOD

A CERTAIN FRAGRANCE—FILLS THE AIR
AS SUMMER TURNS TO FALL
IT TAKES ME BACK TO YESTERYEARS
AND TIMES I STILL RECALL
THE CRISPNESS OF AN EVENING WALK
AS DAYS BEGIN TO WANE
PREPARING FOR A BRAND NEW YEAR
AND GIVING THANKS AGAIN
FOR HOLIDAYS JUST UP AHEAD
WHAT WILL THESE MOMENTS HOLD?
WE PRAY FOR PEACE UPON OUR LAND
AND JOY WITHIN OUR SOULS
THE MEMORIES EMBRACE MY HEART
AS SEASONS COME AND GO
THANK YOU FATHER, FOR EACH DAY
THAT YOU, ALONE, CAN BESTOW.

JILL LEMNING

LORD, HELP ME TO SEE

LORD, HELP ME TO SEE THY MERCY
IN THE RISING OF THE SUN
HELP ME TO ENJOY YOUR LOVE
WHILE LIFE'S RACE I, SWIFTLY, RUN
HELP ME TO SEE YOUR PATIENCE
IN THE RAINDROPS THAT FALL
HELP ME TO SEE YOUR WISDOM
IN EACH THING, LARGE AND SMALL
HELP ME TO SEE YOUR GOODNESS
WHEN THE WORLD IS CAVING IN
LORD, CONSTANTLY, REMIND ME
YOU ARE MY FATHER AND MY FRIEND.

DOTTLEE D. REED

THEREFORE, I WILL LOOK UNTO THE LORD
I WILL WAIT FOR THE GOD OF MY SALVATION, MY GOD WILL HEAR ME.

MICAH 7:7

TAKE TIME

TAKE TIME TO PRAY
TAKE TIME FOR FRIENDS
TAKE TIME FOR WORK
TAKE TIME TO THINK
TAKE TIME TO READ
TAKE TIME TO LAUGH
TAKE TIME TO LOVE
TAKE TIME TO DREAM
TAKE TIME TO PLAY
TAKE TIME TO WORSHIP, IT IS THE
HIGHWAY TO REVERENCE.

AUTHOR UNKNOWN

A QUIET PEACE

TO HEAR THE SOUND
THAT SILENCE MAKES
TO EMBRACE THE STILNESS
THAT WOULD BE EVERYWHERE

NO BEGINNING, BUT,
YET, NO ENDING,
SOME KIND OF UNION
OF HEAVEN AND EARTH'S BLENDING

EMD

I KNOW

I KNOW GOD IS REAL
I KNOW JESUS IS THE WAY
I KNOW THAT I AM HERE
ONLY BECAUSE OF HIM, I PRAY

HE TOOK THE LITTLE OF ME
THE PART THAT IS TRUE
AND LEFT A LITTLE LIGHT
THAT IS MINE EVER MORE

NO LONGER IS IT DARK
IN WAYS THAT SHOULDN'T BE
FOR NOW, BECAUSE OF HIM
I KNOW WHAT IT IS TO BE FREE.

EMD

AN APRIL PRAYER

FORGIVE US LORD
FOR OUR INSECURE, IMMATURE BEHAVIOR
AFTER ALL WE JUST PRETEND,
TO BE GROWN-UPS,
BUT, WHEN THE TRUE TESTS COME, WE ARE
LIKE SMALL CHILDREN, FOR OUR LACK
OF SOUND REASONING.
FORGIVE US, LORD FOR NOT UNDERSTANDING
AND REACTING, INSTEAD OF ACTING, AFTER
ALL, WE ARE STUMBLING, TRYING TO UNDER-
STAND A WORLD THAT PITS PEOPLE AGAINST
TECHNOLOGY AND TECHNOLOGY AGAINST PEOPLE.
ONLY YOU, LORD KNOW WHAT SHOULD, REALLY
BE DONE. HELP US TO BE ABLE, IN ANY
CASE, TO LEAVE THOSE BIG DECISIONS TO
YOU, WHO CAN SEE BEYOND OUR FINITE AND
ERRORFUL WAYS TO A BRIGHTER TOMORROW.

EMD

A WIDOW'S LAST WISH

TO BE CLOSE AGAIN
LIKE ONCE BEFORE
OR TO BE FREE
AS ONE WHO IS SOLO.

TO REMEMBER THE ONE
TIME LIKE NO OTHER
OR TO FORGET THERE
EVER WAS ANOTHER

TO ASK FOR ONE
LAST REY OF LIGHT
BEFORE THE STILLNESS
OF ONE LAST NIGHT

BECOMES THE DAY
TO END ALL DAYS.
THIS IS A WISH
A WIDOW'S LAST WISH

EMD

FOR UNTO US A CHILD IS BORN, UNTO US A SON IS GIVEN AND THE GOVERNMENT SHALL BE UPON HIS SHOULDERS AND HIS NAME SHALL BE CALLED WONDERFUL, COUNSELOR, THE MIGHTY GOD, THE EVERLASTING FATHER, THE PRINCE OF PEACE.

ISAIAH 9:6

THANK YOU DEAR GOD FOR BIRDS THAT SING
FOR BUTTERFLIES WITH SILKEN WING
FOR GOLDEN SUNRISE IN THE SKY
SUNSETS THAT BID THE DAY GOODBYE
THANK YOU, O LORD, FOR RAIN AND SNOW
FOR TREES AND FLOWERS, ALL THAT GROW
WE THANK YOU FOR THE FOOD WE EAT
AND FOR THE SHOES UPON OUR FEET
A SPECIAL THANKS FOR FAMILY LOVE
AND FOR YOUR GUIDANCE FROM ABOVE
PLEASE HELP US LORD WE HUMBLY PRAY
AND REMEMBER YOU WITH THANKS EACH DAY.

RUTH GILLIS

REMEMBER TO PRAY

ASK AND IT SHALL BE GIVEN
SO THE LORD WOULD HAVE YOU PRAY
SEEK AND YOU WILL SURELY FIND
FOR HE WILL SHOW THE WAY
KNOCK AND IT SHALL BE OPENED
DO YOU THINK GOD IS ABOVE
TO TURN HIS BACK UPON YOU,
KNOWING ALL YOU ARE WITHOUT?
WE ARE A LITTLE CHILDREN
IN THIS VALLEY FULL OF TEARS
WE NEED HIS LOVE TO GUIDE US
GIVING MEANING THROUGH THE YEARS
FOR TO CROSS LIFE'S TROUBLED WATERS
THERE IS NO BETTER WAY
THAN CLINGING TIGHTLY TO HIS ARM
AND REMEMBERING TO PRAY.

GRACE E. EASLEY

WHERE WE WILL NEVER GROW OLD

I HAVE HEARD OF A LAND
ON A FAR AWAY STRAND
TIS A BEAUTIFUL HOME OF THE SOUL,
BUILT BY JESUS ON HIGH, THERE,
WE NEVER SHALL DIE.
TIS A LAND WHERE WE NEVER GROW OLD,
NEVER GROW OLD, NEVER GROW OLD
IN A LAND WHERE WE'LL NEVER GROW OLD
NEVER GROW OLD NEVER GROW OLD,
IN A LAND WHERE WE'LL NEVER GROW OLD.

WHEN OUR WORK HERE IS DONE
AND THE LIFE CROWN IS WON
AND OUR TROUBLES AND TRIALS
ARE OVER, ALL OUR SORROW
WILL END AND OUR VOICES WILL
BLEND WITH OUR LOVED ONES, WHO
HAVE GONE ON BEFORE.

NEVER GROW OLD, NEVER GROW OLD,
IN A LAND WHERE WE'LL NEVER GROW OLD

NEVER GROW OLD, NEVER GROW OLD,
IN A LAND WHERE WE'LL NEVER GROW OLD.

JIM REEVES

SWEET HOUR OF PRAYER

WHILE RESTING ONE EVENING
BY THE SIDE OF THE ROAD
I SAW AN OLD FARMER
IN A FIELD HE'D JUST HOED,
HIS FACE WAS ALL BROWN AND WRINKLED
BY THE WIND AND HE WAS TALKING TO
THE LORD, JUST LIKE YOU WOULD
BE TALKING TO A FRIEND.

WELL, SIR, HE SAID IN A VOICE CALM
AND QUIET, THEM CORN TASSELS NEED
SACKING, BUT, I GOT NO STRING TO
TIE IT. HAD NO RAIN IN SO LONG THE
FIELDS ARE MIGHTY DUSTY, AND IT'S
GETTING SO UNBEARABLE HOT, THAT THE
KIDS ARE EVEN FUSSY.

NOW, THAT GRASS DOWN IN THE PASTURE
SHOULD BE KNEE HIGH, IF WE COULD
HAVE A LITTLE SHOWER, LORD, IT MIGHT
KEEP THE COW FROM GOING DRY. Ahh
BUT, LISTEN TO ME TALKING, YOU'D
THINK I WASN'T GRATEFUL. WHY, IF YOU
DIDN'T KNOW ME SO WELL, LORD, YOU'D
THINK I WAS DOWNRIGHT HATEFUL, YOU'D
THINK I'D FORGOT ABOUT THE NEW CALF
AND THE MONEY IN THE MAIL
THAT PAID THE RENT, MAW'S COLD'S BETTER
JOHNNY'S HOME FROM THE NAVY, THAT GOOD
SUNDAY DINNER OF CHICKEN, DUMPLINS AND
GRAVY. THE NEW PREACHER YOU SENT US,
LORD, HE IS A FINE YOUNG MAN. WHY HE'S
JUST CONVERTING SINNERS TO BEAT THE BAND.

(OVER)

(CON'D)

WELL, GUESS I'LL BE MOSING ALONG,
LORD, WON'T TAKE NO MORE OF YOUR TIME.
GUESS THERE'S PLENTY FOLKS, HEREBOUTS,
WAITING TO RING YOUR LINE.

EVENING TO YOU, LORD. WATCH OVER US,
TONIGHT. DON'T WORRY ABOUT US NONE,
LORD, CAUSE EVERYTHING'S GOING TO BE
ALRIGHT.

JIM REEVES

BERRY GORDY, JR. BEGAN BUILDING THE BEST-KNOWN RECORD COMPANY OF THE TWENTIETH CENTURY FROM THE GROUND UP. BY ACCIDENT AND THEN, BY DESIGN, HE DID SO IN AMERICA'S HEARTLAND, AWAY FROM ITS TRADITIONAL MUSIC CAPITALS. GORDY LEARNED THE HARD WAY THAT JAZZ MIGHT NOURISH THE SOUL BUT, IT DIDN'T PAY THE BILLS. FROM THEN ON, 2648 WEST GRAND BLVD. DETROIT, MI BECAME HITSVILLE USA TO MANY ASPIRING YOUNGSTERS. IN 2004, JACK ASHFORD OF FUNK BROTHERS SAID OF THE UNIQUE GORDY APPEAL, "WE RECORDED MUSIC THAT BROUGHT THE WORLD TOGETHER".

ADAM WHITE
MOTOWN RECORDS
UMG RECORDINGS

IN THE GARDEN

I COME TO THE GARDEN, ALONE
WHILE THE DEW IS STILL ON THE ROSES AND
THE VOICE I HEAR, FALLING ON MY EAR
THE SON OF GOD DISCLOSES
AND HE WALKS WITH ME AND HE
TALKS WITH ME AND HE TELLS ME
I AM HIS OWN, AND THE JOY WE SHARE
AS WE TARRY THERE, NONE OTHER
HAS EVER KNOWN.

HE SPEAKS AND THE SOUND OF HIS
VOICE IS SO SWEET, THE BIRDS
HUSH THEIR SINGING

AND THE MELODY THAT HE GAVE TO ME
WITHIN MY HEART, IS RINGING

AND HE WALKS WITH ME AND HE
TALKS WITH ME AND HE TELLS ME
I AM HIS OWN, AND THE JOY
WE SHARE AS WE TARRY THERE,
NONE OTHER HAS EVER KNOWN.

JIM REEVES

IT IS NO SECRET (WHAT GOD CAN DO)

THE CHIMES OF TIME RING OUT THE NEWS
SOMEONE SLIPPED AND FELL
WAS THAT SOMEONE YOU?
YOU MAY HAVE LONGED FOR ADDED
STRENGTH, YOUR COURAGE, TO RENEW,
DO NOT BE DISHEARTENED, I HAVE NEWS
FOR YOU. IT IS NO SECRET WHAT GOD CAN
DO, WHAT HE'S DONE FOR OTHERS, HE'LL
DO FOR YOU, WITH ARMS WIDE OPEN, HE'LL
PARDON YOU, IT IS NO SECRET WHAT GOD
CAN DO.

THERE IS NO NIGHT FOR IN HIS LIGHT
YOU'LL NEVER WALK ALONE, YOU'LL ALWAYS
FEEL AT HOME, WHEREEVER YOU MAY ROAM.
THERE IS NO POWER THAT CAN CONQUER YOU
WHILE GOD IS ON YOUR SIDE, TAKE HIM AT
HIS WORD, DON'T RUN AWAY AND HIDE, IT
IS NO SECRET WHAT GOD CAN DO.

JIM REEVES

PRECIOUS MEMORIES

PRECIOUS MEMORIES
UNSEEN ANGELS
SENT FROM SOMEWHERE TO MY SOUL
HOW THEY LINGER, EVER NEAR ME
THE, THE SACRED PAST UNFOLDS
PRECIOUS MEMORIES, HOW THEY LINGER
HOW THEY EVER FLOOD MY SOUL, IN
THE STILLNESS OF THE MIDNIGHT,
PRECIOUS, SACRED SEAMS UNFOLD
AS I TRAVEL ON LIFE'S PATHWAY, I
KNOW NOT WHAT THE YEARS MAY HOLD
AND AS I PONDER, HOPE GROWS FONDER,
PRECIOUS MEMORIES FLOOD MY SOUL.

JIM REEVES

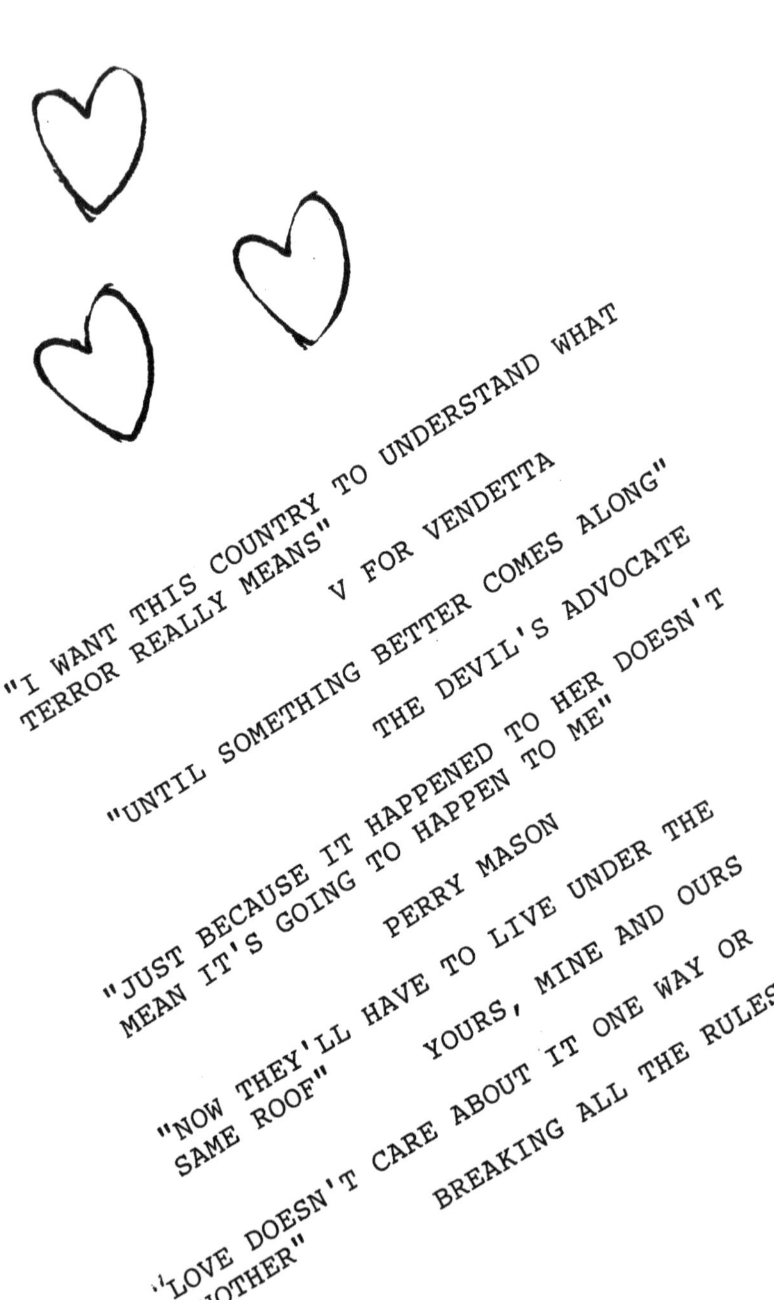
"I WANT THIS COUNTRY TO UNDERSTAND WHAT
TERROR REALLY MEANS"
V FOR VENDETTA
"UNTIL SOMETHING BETTER COMES ALONG"
THE DEVIL'S ADVOCATE
"JUST BECAUSE IT HAPPENED TO HER DOESN'T
MEAN IT'S GOING TO HAPPEN TO ME"
PERRY MASON
"NOW THEY'LL HAVE TO LIVE UNDER THE
SAME ROOF"
YOURS, MINE AND OURS
"LOVE DOESN'T CARE ABOUT IT ONE WAY OR
ANOTHER"
BREAKING ALL THE RULES

THE NIGHTWATCH

GOD'S KEEPING THE NIGHTWATCH
FOR YOU AND ME
BRIGHT STARS ARE WATCHING
THE WORLD, AS IT SLEEPS
SHEPHERDS WATCH OVER
THE LITTLE WHITE SHEEP.

THE LIGHTHOUSE IS SHINING
FOR SHIPS, FAR AT SEA,
AS GOD KEEPS THE NIGHTWATCH
FOR YOU AND FOR ME
SO SLEEP, SLEEP IN PEACE AND REST,
DON'T BE AFRAID OF THE DARKNESS
ALL'S WELL, FOR, OVER THE LAND AND
THE SEA, GOD'S KEEPING THE NIGHTWATCH
FOR YOU AND FOR ME.

JIM REEVES

ANOINTED ONES MAY TAKE THE GOSPEL (PREACH, TEACH, LECTURE, TALK, WRITE)

CHOSEN ONES MAY CARRY THE GOSPEL (YOU ARE NEVER ALONE, SOMEONE WILL BE THERE)

ANYONE MAY SPREAD THE GOSPEL (EVEN BABES, NO ONE'S LEFT OUT)

EMD

Part 2

"YOU CAN TAKE THE GIRL OUT OF THE TRAILER PARK, BUT, YOU CAN'T TAKE THE TRAILER PARK OUT OF THE GIRL"

SWORDFISH

"IT'S NOT THE FIRST TIME I'VE BEEN PROVEN WRONG" SPIDERMAN

WE'RE GONNA HAVE SOME KIND OF RAPPORT, OR WHAT?"

COLORS

"MOMMY, AM I GOING TO DIE?"

SWITCHED AT BIRTH

"YOU'RE GONNA HAVE TO PUT UP WITH ME FOR A VERY LONG TIME"

THE NEXT BEST THING

SAY, FIRST OF GOD, ABOVE OR MAN, BELOW WHAT CAN BE REASON, BUT, FROM WHAT WE KNOW? OF MAN, WHAT SEE WE BUT, HIS STATION HERE, FROM WHICH TO REASON OR TO WHICH REFER? THROUGH WORDS UN-NUMBERED THROUGH THE GOD BE KNOWN, OURS TO TRACE HIM ONLY IN OUR OWN.

(ALEXANDER POPE'S AN ESSAY ON MAN)

TAKE UP THE WHITE MAN'S BURDEN
SEND FORTH THE BEST YE BREED
GO BIND YOUR SONS TO EXILE
TO SERVE YOUR CAPTIVES' NEED
TO WAIT IN HEAVY HARNESS
ON FLUTTERED FOLK AND WILD
YOUR NEW CAUGHT, SULLEN PEOPLES,
HALF-DEVIL AND HALF-CHILD.

(RUDYARD KIPLING'S 'THE WHITE MAN'S BURDEN')

THE WEST WON'T CONTAIN COMMUNISM, IT WILL TRANSCEND COMMUNISM. IT WON'T BOTHER TO DENOUNCE IT, IT WILL DISMISS IT AS SOME BIZARRE CHAPTER IN HUMAN HISTORY WHOSE LAST PAGES ARE EVEN NOW BEING WRITTEN.

(RONALD REAGAN ON COMMUNISM)

FEED ON THAT, THAT IS OF GOD, WASTE NOT ON THAT, THAT IS NOT OF GOD, FOR IT WILL SELF-DESTRUCT, ANYWAY AND THAT, THAT IS OF GOD CANNOT BE DESTROYED.

EMD

TO MY MOTHER, WHO GAVE ME LOVE OF LIFE
TO HILLARY, WHO GAVE ME A LIFE OF LOVE
TO CHELSEA, WHO GAVE JOY AND MEANING
TO IT ALL, AND TO THE MEMORY OF MY
GRANDFATHER, WHO TAUGHT ME TO LOOK UP
TO PEOPLE OTHERS LOOKED DOWN ON BECAUSE WE'RE NOT SO DIFFERENT, AFTERALL.

DEDICATION FROM
'MY LIFE' by PRES.
BILL CLINTON 2004

"AT WELLESLEY, HILLARY HAD DIFINITELY ADOPTED THE POPULAR CONTEMPT FOR CAPITALISM. A COLLEGE BOYFRIEND TOLD DAVID MARANISS, AUTHOR OF 'FIRST IN HIS CLASS,' A BIOGRAPHY OF BILL CLINTON, THAT SHE HAD GROWN UP AND OUT OF THE CONSERVATIVE MATERIALISTIC MIND-SET, WHICH IS TYPICAL OF THE SUBURBS. SHE WAS NOT INTERESTED IN MAKING MONEY OR BEING AFFLUENT. IN HER GRADUATION SPEECH HILLARY STATED "THERE ARE SOME THINGS WE FEEL, FEELINGS THAT OUR PREVAILING, ACQUISITIVE AND COMPETITIVE, CORPORATE LIFE, INCLUDING TRAGICALLY, UNIVERSITIES, IS NOT THE WAY OF LIFE FOR US. WE'RE SEARCHING FOR MORE IMMEDIATE ECSTATIC AND PENETRATING MODES OF LIVING. "HOW EASY IT IS TO SAY THESE WORDS, BUT, AS WE SHALL SEE HOW DIFFICULT IT IS TO LIVE BY THEM."

("SHE TOOK A VILLAGE"
by ALAN GOTTLIEBE)

INTERVIEW WITH A PRESIDENT: QUESTIONS I WOULD ASK THE PRESIDENT.

YOU WERE KIND OF AWKWARD AS A KID. QUESTIONS: YOU BROKE YOUR LEG ABOVE THE KNEE AS A KID. WAS IT THE SAME LEG THAT YOU FELL AND HURT THAT LANDED YOU IN THE HOSPITAL, AS PRESIDENT?

YOU DIDN'T KNOW YOUR OWN FATHER, BUT, BOTH OF YOUR STEP FATHERS LOVED YOU AND YOUR MOTHER AND YOU LOVED THEM, AS MUCH. DID YOU, CONSCIOUSLY, MISS YOUR OWN DAD?

SOMETHING MORE POISONOUS THAN ALCOHOL DROVE YOUR STEP FATHER, CLINTON, TO THE LEVEL OF DEBASEMENT. DO YOU BLAME THAT OR ANY SIMILAR CIRCUMSTANCE OR CONDITIONS RELATED TO GROWING UP IN THE SOUTHERN PART OF THE UNITED STATES?

ON THIRTEENTH STREET IN HOPE, YOU WERE INTRODUCED TO MOVIES. YOU COULD GO TO THE MOVIES WITH FRIENDS OR ALONE. MOVIES WERE A NICKEL, COKES, A NICKEL. YOUR FAVORITE MOVIE WAS HIGH NOON. WERE YOU ATTRACTED TO GUNS AS A KID?

THINKING OF THE LOOK IN GARY COOPER'S EYES, AS HE STARED INTO THE FACE OF, ALMOST, CERTAIN DEFEAT. DID HIS, (G.C.) DEAD DETERMINATION TO FACE HIS ADVERSARY, PREMANENTLY, INFLUENCE YOU, AT ANY TIME IN REAL LIFE?

YOU TOOK YOUR STEP COUSIN, KARLA, OUT IN THE FIELDS TO SEE THE SHEEP AND YOU YOURSELF WERE RAMMED. WAS THAT A LESSON FOR YOU?

WHAT DO YOU MEAN BY "WHEN BRAVE SOULS RAGE AGAINST THE DYING OF THE LIGHT"?

WHAT KEPT YOU FROM GETTING TO KNOW SUPREME COURT JUSTICE, CLARENCE THOMAS?

YOU VALUE SOLITUDE. DID YOU EVER SEE YOURSELF A CONFIRMED BACHELOR?

WHAT DO YOU THINK OF INTERRACIAL MARRIAGES, LIKE JUSTICE THOMAS?

AFTER READING C. VAN WOODWARD'S "THE BURDEN OF SOUTHERN HISTORY", NOTING SOUTHRENERS' PECULIAR HISTORICAL CONSCIOUSNESS, HOW WERE YOU, PERSONALLY, TOUCHED? DO YOU FEEL THE LABEL, 'SOUTHERNER' IS, IN ITSELF, BIAS, EVEN THOUGH, NOT RACIALLY, BIASED? DO YOU FEEL YOU WERE ADVANTAGED BY BEING BORN IN ARKANSAS RATHER THAN LOUISIANA, GEORGIA, ALABAMA OR MISSISSIPPI? IF SO, IN WHAT WAY? DO YOU FEEL EACH STATE HAS IT'S OWN STORY TO TELL, SOME BEING MORE BIASED THAN OTHERS? HOW DO YOU FEEL ABOUT THE TERM, "POOR WHITE TRASH"?

YOU AND YOUR WIFE WERE LAW PARTNERS. YOU MENTION THAT THE TWO OF YOU WERE PROSECUTORS IN STATE V. PORTER. YOU DESCRIBE THE VICTIM AS A 'LONG-HAIRED KID'. PORTER IS A POLICEMAN, ACCUSED OF BEATING THE KID TO DEATH. YOU STATE YOU HAD AN 'OFF' DAY IN THE TRIAL AND HILLARY HAD POOR TASTE IN COURTROOM ATTIRE. DO YOU CONSIDER YOUR WIFE AND YOURSELF, GOOD ATTORNEYS?

DO YOU THINK YOU WOULD BE BETTER LEGAL PROFESSIONALS IF YOU PRACTICED SEPARATELY? OR ON SEPARATE LAW FIRMS? YOU LOST THE CASE AGAINST THE POLICEMAN. DID YOU AND HILLARY DO ALL THAT YOU COULD TO VINDICATE THE KIDS LIFE OR TO SEE THAT JUSTICE WAS SERVED? IF THE DEFENDANT HAD NOT BEEN A COP DO YOU THINK THAT YOU AND HILLARY WOULD HAVE WON THE CASE? SHOULD WE ASSUME THAT, BY YOUR DESCRIPTION, THAT THE VICTIM WAS A WHITE MALE?

DO YOU THINK THAT YOU COULD HAVE MET A 'HILLARY' IN ARKANSAS? YOUR MOM WAS SIX MONTHS PREGNANT WITH YOU WHEN YOUR DAD DIED. DO YOU FEEL YOU COULD HAVE BEEN BORN TO SEE YOUR DAD IF YOUR MOTHER HAD GONE INTO LABOR BEFORE YOUR FATHER'S DEATH? DO YOU FEEL THE FETUS, AT THAT TIME, IS A BABY THAT YOU WOULD WANT TO BE AND BE BORN AFTER, ONLY SIX MONTHS PRENATAL OR DO YOU FEEL WE SHOULD HOLD OUT FOR NINE MONTHS FOR ADEQUATE TIME FOR COMPLETE FORMATION AND DEVELOPMENT? HUMAN LIFE BEGINS AT THE MOMENT OF BIRTH, NOT CONCEPTION. YOU ARE A CHRISTIAN. THAT MEANS YOU WANT TO TAKE FULL ADVANTAGE OF POSITIVE OPPORTUNITIES, BOTH SPIRITUALLY AND SECULARLY, AS FAR AS YOUR LIFE IN THIS WORLD IS CONCERNED. SCRIPTURE STATES THAT 'IN THE FULLNESS OF TIME, HE SENT FORTH HIS SON INTO THE WORLD.

AT THIS TIME, HE WAS WORTHY TO BECOME THE SACRIFICE, NEEDED TO REMOVE THE SINS OF SEPARATION. ANYTIME SOONER, HE WOULD NOT HAVE BEEN AS WORTHY. PERHAPS NOT WORTHY ENOUGH TO BECOME SAVIOUR OF THE PEOPLE IN NEED OF ONE. DO YOU FEEL IT IS CRUEL AND INHUMAN PUNISHMENT TO EXPECT A FETUS TO DO AT SIX MONTHS, WHAT A FUL-TERM BABY IS EXPECTED TO DO? IN OTHER WORDS, HUMANITY RECEIVES THE BABY THE INSTANCE IT APPEARS OUTSIDE THE MOTHER'S BODY AND THE MOTHER CEASES TO BE A MOTHER-TO-BE AND BECOMES A MOTHER. SHE IS NO LONGER HOST TO THE LIFE INSIDE HER FOR THAT LIFE IS, NOW A FULLY, FORMED AND DEVELOPED INFANT AND READY FOR THE WORLD. DO YOU AGREE? WHAT DO THE TERMS "PRO LIFE AND PRO CHOICE" MEAN TO YOU AS A CHRISTIAN? DO YOU INTEND TO FATHER A SON? OR DO YOU FEEL YOUR PARENTING IS COMPLETE WITH CHELSEA?

BEFORE CHIEF JUSTICE, WILLIAM REHNQUIST DIED, HE SWORE IN PRESIDENT GEORGE BUSH FOR A SECOND TERM. DO YOU THINK JOHN KERRY EVER HAD A CHANCE, BEYOND HIS NOMINATION, TO BECOME PRESIDENT OR DO YOU THINK HIS WAS A SYMPATHETIC CAMPAIGN BASED ON THE PUBLIC'S STRONG AWARENESS OF INTEREST IN HEALTH CARE, ESPECIALLY, SERIOUS ILLNESSES, SUCH AS, CANCER, WHICH JOHN KERRY, BOB DOLE, RONALD REAGAN AND CHIEF JUSTICE REHNQUIST, ALL, SHARED.?

DURING MR. BUSH'S CAMPAIGN FOR A SECOND TERM, HE WAS HEARD MAKING THE REMARK 'BRING IT ON', CONCERNING THE POTENTIAL OUTBREAK OF A FULL FLEDGE WAR IN IRAQ. EVEN HIS WIFE, LAURA, IS SAID TO HAVE CAUTIONED HIS REMARK. DO YOU THINK THIS KIND OF ATTITUDE HELPED HIM IN GETTING HIS SECOND TERM? DO YOU THINK IT WOULD BE PSYCHOLOGICALLY, AS WELL AS POLITICALLY CORRECT, TO SAY THAT MR. BUSH'S WARLIKE OR BELIGERENT ATTITUDE WON OVER MR. KERRY'S MORE FORMAL MILITARY EXPERIENCE?

HOW DO YOU FEEL, BOTH, PRESONALLY AND POLITICALLY, ABOUT BURDENING THE PEOPLE OF AMERICA WITH TWENTY YEARS, TWO DECADES, A SCORE OF DEEP SOUTH PRESIDENTIAL DYNASTY? DO YOU THINK THAT THE BUSH-CLINTON-BUSH DYNASTY HAS DONE ANYTHING TO HELP UNITE THE COUNTRY IN SPITE OF NEGATIVE PRECONCEIVED IDEAS ABOUT THE DEEP SOUTH?

IS REVEREND GRAHAM ONE, YOU WOULD CONSIDER A SPIRITUAL ROLE MODEL ANY WHERE IN THE WORLD, SIMILAR TO THE POPE? IN MY OPINION, ONE IS A SPIRITUAL ROLE MODEL AND THE OTHER IS A RELIGIOUS LEADER. WOULD YOU AGREE?

WHAT, IN PARTICULAR, SCARED THE LIVING HELL OUT OF YOU UPON DISCOVERING YOURSELF DURING JUNIOR HIGH SCHOOL? WHY WERE YOU ANGRY AT YOUR DAD? DO YOU UNDERSTAND MORE, NOW, ABOUT WHY GOD DOES WHAT HE DOES, NOW THAT YOU ARE MORE MATURE?

HERE-TO-FORE, I HAVE ASKED QUESTIONS BASED ON SITUATIONS YOU MENTION IN YOU AUTOBIOGRAPHY. NOW, I AM POSING QUESTIONS THAT I WOULD ASK OF ANY ONE OF THE PRESIDENTS? DO YOU THINK THAT FIRST LADIES OF THE WHITE HOUSE SHOULD STRIVE TO HAVE DISTINCT PUBLIC PERSONALITIES OF THEIR OWN APART FROM THEIR HUSBAND'S POSITIONS OR SHOULD THEY BE CONTENT TO BE SEEN AS A PART OF ONLY, WHAT THE PRESIDENT DOES?

SOME FORMER FIRST LADIES HAVE MADE MEMORABLE IMPRINTS OF THEIR OWN, WHILE IN THE WHITE HOUSE THAT LEND TO THEIR DISTINCT PUBLIC PERSONALITIES, SUCH AS JACKIE KENNEDY AND HER KEEN EYE FOR STYLE AND DECORUM, BETTYE FORD'S PERSONAL INTEREST IN SUBSTANCE ABUSE AND ADDICTIVE SUBSTANCES, AND EVERYBODY WILL RECALL THE IMPACT THAT HILLARY CLINTON MADE ON THE ISSUE OF HEALTH CARE AND MAKING IT AVAILABLE TO CHILDREN AND THE DISADVANTAGED.

DO YOU FEEL THAT THE DYNASTY (DIE-NASTY) MAY HAVE DONE MORE TO BROADEN THE GAP AS FAR AS UNDERSTANDING THE DIFFERENCES, WHETHER PERCEIVED OR ACTUAL, IN ATTITUDES PERTAINING TO THE SOUTH AS OPPOSED TO THOSE OF THE REST OF THE COUNTRY?

DO YOU FEEL THAT HURRICANE KATRINA COULD HAVE HAPPENED WITHOUT THE DYNASTY IN PLACE? CAN WE SEE THE HURRICANE AS A PERMANENT MARKING IN OUR OWN COUNTRY OF THE DAMAGES THAT WARS, ANYWHERE CAN HAVE ON THE SECURITY OF A COUNTRY?

TO SEE THE HAND OF GOD IN THE HURRICANE DISASTER IS TO SEE THE HAND OF GOD EVERYWHERE FOR ALL TIME. CAN WE SEE THIS AS SOME SORT OF WARNING THAT WE SHOULD NOT TAKE THE BLESSINGS OF GOD LIGHTLY OR FOR GRANTED? AFTERALL, WE STARTED OUT TO MAKE A DEAL WITH NAPOLEON FOR ONLY A SMALL PART OF WEST FLORIDA AND A PART OF NEW ORLEANS AND WOUND UP WITH, WHAT, IS NOW, TEXAS, NEW MEXICO, OKLAHOMA, LOUISIANA, ARK-ANSAS, MISSOURI, IOWA, MINNESOTA, NORTH DAKOTA, SOUTH DAKOTA, NEBRASKA, KANSAS, COLORADO, WYOMING AND MONTANA. I WOULD CALL THIS A BLESSING, AS WELL AS A BARGAIN FOR FIFTEEN MILLION DOLLARS. IT IS AN EVEN BETTER DEAL THAN THE ACQUISITION OF MANHATTEN, SINCE THE DEAL DOUBLED THE UNITED STATES' GEOGRAPHICAL AREA. I FEEL NAPOLEON AND THE INDIANS WOULD AGREE THAT WE WERE, INDEED, BLESSED IN THE BARGAINS.

YOU APPROVED THE FIRST EXECUTIONS IN ARKANSAS, SINCE 1964. COULD YOU VOTE TO ABOLISH THE DEATH PENALTY IN THE UNITED STATES? THERE WAS A TIME, IN THE SOUTH, WHEN IT WAS SAFE TO LEAVE YOUR HOME UNLOCKED, EVEN WHILE YOU WERE SLEEPING. YOU TRAVEL ABROAD FREQUENTLY. THERE ARE STILL PLACES WHERE NEIGHBORS TRUST EACH OTHER ENOUGH TO LEAVE DOORS UNLOCKED. DO YOU RECALL ANY PLACES IN PARTICULAR WHERE PEOPLE TRUST EACH TO THIS EX-TENT?

YOU COMPLETED A SPEECH BY SAYING, "WE ARE HERE TO SAVE AMERICA". WHAT DO YOU MEAN? IF AMERICA IS THE CIVILIZED BEACON THAT THE REST OF THE WORLD SEES, WHY THE URGENCY TO SAVE AMERICA?

YOUR WIFE COMES TO YOUR DEFENSE ON OCCASION. IS THIS SOLELY UP TO HER WHEN SHE SHOULD INTERVENE? WAS GEN-NIFER FLOWERS, EVER, CONSIDERED A THREAT TO YOURS AND HILLARY'S RE-LATIONSHIP? YOU HAVE IMPROVED IN YOUR, OVERALL, POLITICAL MATURITY AND ARE NO LONGER DESCRIBED AS HAVING HAD BREAKFAST AT I-HOP, ONCE. DO YOU THINK YOUR ABILITY TO FORGIVE AND FORGET WAS NESCESSARY FOR YOU TO COME THIS FAR? DO YOU, STILL, BLAME YOUR DAD FOR ANYTHING? DO YOU FEEL FATHERING ONE CHILD AND BEING WITH-OUT A FATHER OF YOUR OWN LIMITS YOU QUALIFICATIONS TO SAY HOW OTHER AMERICANS SHOULD CONDUCT THEIR PARENTAL AFFAIRS?

AFFIRMATIVE ACTION IS POLICY, WHEREBY, SOME OLD 'SLIGHTS' ARE CORRECTED, BY A SORT OF STEPPED-UP, MUTUALLY AGREED UPON, WAY TO PRODUCE FEWER DISPARITIES IN, AT LEAST, THE VERY BASICS, THAT SOCIETY HAS TO OFFER, SUCH AS, AFFORDABLE HOUSING, HEALTHCARE AND EMPLOYMENT OPPORTUNITIES. IN OTHER WORDS, PROCEDURES, THAT ALLOW FOR CLOSING THE GAPS THAT EXIST FOR SOME, BROUGHT ABOUT BY DISCRIMINATION BY OTHERS IN A MORE DELIBERATE OR DIRECT MANNER. DO YOU FEEL THESE DISPARITIES CAN BE COMPLETELY ELIMINATED OR SHOULD WE SETTLE FOR A 'CATCHING-UP' AND NOT REACH FOR SOMETHING THAT IS NOT FORTHCOMING?

BEFORE THE SIGNING OF THE EMANCIPATION PROCLAMATION, ONE OF THE PROBLEMS OF THE PEOPLE WAS THAT SOME WHITES WERE POOR, ALSO. ESSENTIALLY, THERE WERE THREE GROUPS INVOLVED. THAT WAS BLACKS, WHITES AND POOR WHITES. BEING AN IRISH PROTESTANT, HOW WOULD YOU HAVE HANDLED THE SITUATION?

"GIVE THEM A CLEAR MIND, A WARM HEART, CALMNESS IN THE MIDST OF TURMOIL, REASSURANCE IN TIMES OF DISCOURAGEMENT AND YOUR PRESENCE ALWAYS." THIS IS A STATEMENT MADE BY YOUR FRIEND, REV. BILLY GRAHAM. DO YOU AGREE WITH HIM IN HIS STATEMENT CONCERNING THE PEOPLE?

DO YOU CONSIDER YOUR LEGAL EXPERTISE BETTER AS SEEN IN PUBLIC DEFENDER-TYPE CASES AS THOSE WITH DEFENDANTS TOO POOR, FINANCIALLY, TO AFFORD MORE EXPENSIVE COUNSEL? WILL YOU MAKE THIS TYPE WORK A LARGE PART OF YOUR POST PRESIDENTIAL YEARS? NOBODY, BUT, NOBODY COULD DISLIKE EX PRESIDENT JIMMY CARTER. DO YOU FEEL HE COULD HAVE BEEN ELECTED PRESIDENT, HAD HE BEEN FROM SOME OTHER PART OF THE U.S.?

I DROVE A NEW LITTLE YELLOW FIAT (I PREFERRED IT TO A VOLKSWAGON) IN THE BERKELEY, CALIFORNIA AREA FOR TWO OR THREE YEARS AND THOUGHT THE CAR WAS A LITTLE JEWEL, EXCEPT FOR HILL OR MOUNTAIN CLIMBING. I USED IT MAINLY TO JITNEY MYSELF AROUND WITH THREE KIDS IN SCHOOL. HOW DID HILLARY GET BY WITH A FIAT IN THE OZARKS?

IS DAVID DUKE A PERSONAL FRIEND OF YOURS? DID IT BOTHER YOU THAT SOME SAW ARKANSAS AS THE HOME OF THE KKK? DOES MONICA LEWINSKY REMIND YOU OF YOUR MOTHER IN PHYSICAL APPEARANCE? IT HAS BEEN SAID THAT ONE OF YOUR FAULTS IS THAT YOU SEE SO MUCH THAT NEEDS TO BE DONE WHEREEVER YOU ARE. DO YOU EVER FEEL CAUGHT UP ENOUGH TO REALLY SEE YOURSELF RETIRED ONE DAY? DO YOU FEEL IT IS POSSIBLE TO REACH BEYOND YOUR GRASP AND MAYBE THIS HAS SOMETHING TO DO WITH YOUR SEEING THINGS UNFINISHED MOST OF THE TIME?

YOU QUOTED ABRAHAM LINCOLN. WAS HE A PERSONAL FAVORITE PRESIDENT OF YOURS? MR. LINCOLN SEEMED TO DISPLAY HIS TRUST IN GOD VERY EASILY. YOU SHOW A BELIEF IN GOD. DO YOU FIND IT HARD TO TRUST GOD?

UPON REDECORATING THE WHITE HOUSE AFTER YOU MOVED YOUR FAMILY IN, YOU MENTION AN ANTIQUE TABLE THAT BELONGED TO MARY TODD LINCOLN AND YOUR C.D.'S. PEOPLE OF FINANCIAL STATUS ARE SAID TO HAVE CERTIFICATE OF DEPOSITS AND THOSE WITHOUT FINANCIAL CLOUT HAVE COMPACT DISCS. WHICH DO YOU HAVE?

YOUR WIFE CHOOSES HER HAIRDRESSER. YOU SEEM CANDID, TO A FAULT. HAVE YOU BEEN TOLD THIS BEFORE? DO YOU SIILL PREFER TO FACE DOMESTIC ISSUES AS OPPOSED TO FOREIGN POLICY? "IN THE DESERTS OF THE HEART, LET THE HEALING FOUNTAINS START", DON'T YOU FEEL THIS IS A UNIVERSAL MESSAGE, THAT SHOULD BE UNDERSTOOD BY ALL? DO POLITICS COMPLICATE, ONLY, TO SIMPLIFY?

MANY FEEL BLACKS CANNOT ATTAIN WEALTH IN AMERICA AND MUST BE SATISFIED WITH MIDDLE CLASS STATUS AS THEY ARE SATISFIED WITH BEING BLACK. IN OTHER WORDS, THE INFERIOR STIGMA IS REMOVED BUT, THE BLACK LABEL REMAINS. DO YOU AGREE?

CORA WALTERS, YOUR SITTER OR HOUSEKEEPER, WORKED FOR YOU FOR ELEVEN YEARS. SHE WAS A GOOD CHRISTIAN WOMAN, AS WAS HER WHOLE FAMILY. AFTER SHE LEFT AS YOUR HOUSEKEEPER, MAYE HIGHTOWER CAME TO WORK AND STAYED THIRTY MORE YEARS UNTIL YOUR MOM DIED. CORA WAS A TOUGH OLD GAL AND HELPED YOU KILL A HUGE RAT ONCE. WHAT WOMAN INFLUENCED YOU THE MOST IN CHOOSING A WIFE OR DO YOU FEEL IT WAS A PART OF DESTINY THAT HILLARY SHARE YOUR LIFE?

YOU LOVED TO READ AND SPELL IN SCHOOL AND OFTEN GOT STRAIGHT A'S IN THESE STUDIES, BUT, YOU RECEIVED C'S IN CONDUCT. DO YOU THINK YOU WERE SHOWING SIGNS OF BECOMING 'TOO SOCIALABLE'?

GEORGE LEOPOULAS WAS ONE OF YOUR BEST GREEK FRIENDS. YOU SAW BRIDGE STREET AT HOME AS THE SHORTEST STREET IN AMERICA. DO YOU, STILL FEEL IT IS THE COUNTRY'S SHORTEST STREET?

YOU LIVED NEXT TO THE PERRY PLAZA MOTEL IN YOUR HOMETOWN AND LIKED THE PERRY'S DAUGHTER, TAVIA, WHO WAS A YEAR OR TWO OLDER THAN YOU. SHE SHOT YOU WITH A BB GUN IN THE LEG. WAS THIS THE SAME LEG YOU BROKE EARLIER AS A KID? WAS IT THE SAME ONE YOU BROKE AS PRESIDENT? DO YOU BELIEVE IN CURSES? DO YOU BELIEVE THERE IS SUCH A THING AS CURSE? THE 'SEER' YOU ENCOUNTERED LATER, WAS HIS PREDICTION INFLUENTIAL ON YOUR LATER DECISIONS AND ASPIRATIONS?

YOUR UNCLE ROY SERVED ONE TERM IN A LEGISLATIVE POSITION. YOU HANDED OUT CARDS OR LEAFLETS IN YOUR NEIGHHOOD FOR HIM. WOULD YOU CONSIDER THIS YOUR FIRST EXPERIENCE AT CAMPAIGNING FOR YOURSELF OR ANYONE ELSE?

DID GOVERNOR ORVAL FAUBUS INFLUENCE YOU IN STATE GOVERNMENT? WOULD YOU HAVE REACTED THE SAME WAY IF YOU WERE GOVERNOR AT THE TIME OF THE SUPREME COURT'S LITTLE ROCK CENTRAL HIGH DECISION INVOLVING THE, SO-CALLED 'LITTLE ROCK NINE'?

TELEVISION, IN THE EARLY FIFTIES, INCLUDED SHOWS, LIKE HOWDY-DOWDY, CAP'N KANGAROO, BUFFALO BOB SMITH, ETC. DO YOU FEEL TELEVISION POLITICS INFLUENCED YOUR DECISION TO FOLLOW A CAREER IN POLITICS?

YOU LOVE ELVIS PRESLEY. IS THERE ANYONE, THAT YOU KNOW, PERSONALLY, THAT YOU DON'T LOVE? IS LOVING EASY OR TOUGH FOR YOU? SOME PEOPLE REFER TO JEHOVAH'S WITNESSES AS DEVILS. WHAT DO YOU THINK OF CULTS OR SECTS SUCH AS THE BRANCH DIVIDIANS?

YOU MENTION THE WORD DEMONIZED IN SEVERAL PLACES IN YOUR STORY. WHAT DOES THE WORD, DEMONIZE MEAN TO YOU? DO YOU FEEL YOU SHOULD USE SUCH A WORD IN DESCRIBING, OTHERWISE, FAIR POLITICS? WHAT WAS YOUR EARLIEST EXPERIENCE WITH DEMONS OR DEMONIZING?

TOMMY O'NEAL SAID THAT HE COULD REMEMBER WHEN HE WAS BORN. DO YOU TRY TO CONSCIOUSLY, ASSOCIATE YOUR PRENATAL EXISTENCE WITH YOUR REAL FATHER'S DEATH?

YOU ADORED YOUR SIXTH GRADE TEACHER, KATHLEEN SCHAER, WHO, ALONG WITH HER COUSIN, WERE SPINSTERS AND BELIEVED IN 'TOUGH LOVE'. WHAT IS TOUGH LOVE?

YOUR PARENTS DIDN'T ATTEND CHURCH OFTEN, BUT, ENCOURAGED YOU TO DO SO. YOU LEARNED YOU WERE A SINNER AND NEEDED A SAVIOUR. SO YOU MADE AN OPENPROFESSION OF FAITH AT PARK PLACE BAPTIST CHURCH AND ACCEPTED CHRIST AS YOUR SAVIOUR AND WAS BAPTISED AND BECAME A FAITHFUL MEMBER. DO YOU FEEL YOU WERE, SPIRITUALLY, CALLED AND YOU DEDICATED YOUR LIFE TO THIS CALLING, MAINLY, TO HELP OTHERS? YOU WERE GIFTED. DO YOU FEEL YOU HAVE THE GIFT OF 'HELPS'? DO YOU FEEL YOUR SIPIRITUAL CALLING WAS OR IS ABOVE OR GOES BEYOND EVERYDAY POLITICS?

YOUR WIFE, HILLARY IS METHODIST AND THIS IS A RESULT OF HER BEING "SPRINKLED' AS A BABY INSTEAD OF FULL WATER BAPTISM AS THAT OF BAPTISTS. WHICH FAITH DO YOU AND YOUR FAMILY (HILLARY AND CHELSEA) EMBRACE? WHAT DOES HELL MEAN TO YOU?

DO YOU SEE JESUS AS A MAN WITH A SENSE OF HUMOR? WHAT IS A SENSE OF HUMOR WORTH IN THE WORLD OF POLITICS TO A PRESIDENT?

SOME EXAMPLES OF WHAT MANKIND SHOULD BE ARE SOUTHERNERS. DO YOU AGREE? DO YOU FEEL YOU ARE ONE.

1957 IS A MEMORABLE YEAR FOR ME. I GRADUATED FROM HIGH SCHOOL IN 1957 IN LOUISIANA. THE LITTLE ROCK NINE, OF THAT YEAR , MADE HISTORICAL MENTION. WERE THE SAME LITTLE ROCK NINE ALIVE WHEN YOU BECAME GOVERNOR? DID YOU INVITE THE SAME LITTLE ROCK NINE TO THE GOVERNOR'S MANSION IN 1987?

WAS ELIZABETH ECKFORD AND HAZEL MASSERY'S PRESENCE ANY DIFFERENT WITH GOVERNOR HUCKABEE IN 1997 THAN WITH GOVERNOR FAUBUS IN 1957? DID EACH ONE OF THE ORIGINAL LITTLE ROCK CENTRAL HIGH NINE RECEIVE A CONGRESSIONAL MEDAL OF HONOR WHEN YOU WERE PRESIDENT?

IN 1957, YOU ENJOYED RIDING THE TRAILWAYS BUS, AS YOU WOULD EAT LOTS OF THE LITTLE SANDWICHES THAT THE ATTENDANTS SERVED. TRAILWAYS BUS RIDES WERE UNEVENTFUL FOR YOU, AS FAR AS SEPARATION OF THE RACES IN SEATING WAS CONCERNED. WHAT DID YOU THINK OF THE SEATING ON THE BUSES AT THAT TIME? WHAT DID YOU THINK OF ROSA PARK'S BUS SITUATION THAT LED TO THE INTERGRATED SEATING ARRANGEMENTS ON CITY BUSES?

YOU LOVED BILLY GRAHAM. DID YOU EVER THINK OF BECOMING A PREACHER OR MINISTER OF THE GOSPEL AFTER YOUR PUBLIC PROFESSION OF FAITH IN CHURCH?

DO YOU FEEL IT IS SIGNIFICANT TO SEE THE 911 TRAGEDY IN MANHATTEN AND THE TRAGEDY IN NEW ORLEANS, AS A SORT OF WARNING TO BE EVER THANKFUL, PROUD, BUT, WITH HONESTY AND HUMILITY. FOR WE STAND ON THE LAND THAT WAS PURCHASED WHEN HUMILITY WAS WORTH AS MUCH OR MORE THAN U.S. DOLLARS AS EVIDENCED BY THE SHOW OF LOVE AND AFFECTION BETWEEN TWO GREAT MEN OF DIFFERING POLITICAL APPEAL, THOMAS JEFFERSON AND JOHN ADAMS. ASIDE FROM JESUS AND JOHN; ROMEO AND JULIET, A SHOW OF MORE PUBLIC AFFECTION IS RARELY SEEN THAN WHEN THE TWO MEN EMBRACED EACH OTHER, ALMOST IN DEATH. IT'S WITH THIS KIND OF HUMILITY THAT WE BRING, WITH THANKS, FOR A COUNTRY FOUNDED ON THE UNDYING PRINCIPLES OF LOVE AND CONCERN FOR EACH OTHER. END OF INTERVIEW.

EMD

THE AMERICAN SOUND IS HOPEFUL, BIG-HEARTED, IDEALISTIC, DARING, DECENT AND FAIR. THAT'S OUR HERITAGE. THAT'S OUR SONG.

RONALD REAGAN
2nd INAUGURATION 1985

MAY WE NEVER FORGET THAT IN THE SUNSHINE OF OUR LIVES, THROUGH THE STORM AND AFTER THE RAIN, IT IS ALL WITH GOD IN ALL WAYS AND FOREVER.

JOHN COLTRANE
"A LOVE SUPREME"

IT IS A GOOD CANVAS, ON WHICH SOME STROKES, ONLY, WANT RETOUCHING.

THOMAS JEFFERSON
(COMMENTING ON THE FIRST DRAFT OF THE U.S. CONSTITUTION)

I THINK THIS IS THE MOST EXTRAORDINARY COLLECTION OF TALENT, ON HUMAN KNOWLEDGE THAT HAS EVER BEEN GATHERED TOGETHER AT THE WHITE HOUSE, WITH THE POSSIBLE EXCEPTION OF WHEN THOMAS JEFFERSON DINED ALONE.

PRESIDENT J.F. KENNEDY
(OF THE WHITE HOUSE GATHERING, HONORING NOBEL PRIZE WINNERS IN 1967)

WE HAVE, THIS, MORNING, WITNESSED ONE OF THE MOST INTERESTING SCENES A FREE PEOPLE CAN EVER WITNESS. THE CHANGES OF ADMINISTRATION, WHICH IN EVERY GOVERNMENT AND IN EVERY AGE HAVE MOST GENERALLY, BEEN EPOCHS OF CONFUSION, VILLAINY AND BLOODSHED, IN THIS OUR HAPPY COUNTRY, TAKE PLACE, WITHOUT ANY SPECIES OF DISTRACTION OR DISORDER.

(OBSERVER AT THE INAUGURATION OF THOMAS JEFFERSON)

LET US NOT FEAR, TO NEGOTIATE, BUT, LET US, NOT NEGOTIATE TO FEAR.

ASK NOT, WHAT YOUR COUNTRY CAN DO FOR YOU, BUT ASK WHAT YOU CAN DO FOR YOUR COUNTRY.

JOHN F. KENNEDY

I WILL LEAD AND I WILL DO THE BEST THAT I CAN.

LYNDON B. JOHNSON

LET US MEASURE WHAT WE WILL DO FOR OTHERS BY WHAT OTHERS CAN DO FOR THEMSELVES.

RICHARD M. NIXON

I AM INDEBTED TO NO MAN, ONLY ONE WOMAN.

GERALD R. FORD

WE SEEK A PEACE THAT WILL ENDURE FOR GENERATIONS TO COME, A BETTER WAY TO PEACE, A BETTER WAY TO PROGRESS.

RICHARD M. NIXON

GOD, HELPING ME, I WILL NOT LET YOU DOWN.

GERALD R. FORD

BY OUR IDEALS, MANY HAVE ACHIEVED THEIR FREEDOM.

GEORGE W. BUSH

"THIS PLACE IS HAUNTED BY A WITCH"

THE BROTHERS GRIMM

"I WANT TO KNOW WHAT KIND OF PANCAKES
TO ORDER YOU IN THE MORNING"

A NIGHT AT THE ROXBURY

"WE LIVED FOR LUST, LOVE AND BEAUTY"

DANGEROUS BEAUTY

'WE'VE BEEN CHASING THIS MAN FOR THE LAST
SIX MONTHS" U.S. MARSHALLS

"HE DOESN'T DESERVE TO BE A FATHER"

WITCH HUNT

"EVERY LITTLE KID WANTS A BIRTHDAY PARTY"

LITTLE MAN TATE

"I HAVE TWO GIRLFRIENDS IN THE BAR"

CHARLIE'S ANGELS, FULL THROTTLE

R

Hamilton

Johnson

Jefferson

Wash.ngton

Reagan

John Adams

Nixon

"JOINING THE NOBLES IS THE ONLY HOPE FOR OUR PEOPLE" BRAVEHEART

"DARLING, HE'S NOT GOING TO HURT ME" LAKE PLACID

TO A BEAUTY

YOU WHO ARE BLESSED INCOMPARABLE, UNSURPASSED, SO CARELESSLY PERFECT IN BEAUTY AND GRACE, SO CHASTE AND ETHEREAL IN THOUGHT AND DEMEANOR IN ALL YOU WAYS.

YOU WERE SITTING, UNAWARE OF NOT BEING ALONE, PENSIVELY THE STRINGS THE WHILE. YOUR WHITE ARMS AND SILK LIKE SLEEVES TRAIL THE CHIN AND ON YOUR LIPS, A SMILE.

THE MELODY STOPPED AND YOU GLANCED AT THE VIEW OF LENGTHENING EVENING SHADOWS ON THE PLAINS. YOU COULD NOT HAVE KNOWN, FOR YOU NEVER KNEW A MAN IN CHAINS.

O HAPPY ONE, IF I COULD TELL YOU ALL MY LONGING, THE ENVIOUS THOUGHT OF ALL THE THINGS THAT YOU OWN, THE HUMBLEST OBJECTS, CLOSE TO YOU, THAT BELONG TO YOU, ALONE.

I WOULD BE THE ROUGE THAT KISSES YOUR LIPS, THE COLLAR THAT BRUSHES YOUR FRAGRANT HAIR, THE GIRDLE THAT EMBRACES YOUR GENTLE WAIST, YOUR SHOES THAT FOLLOW YOUR STEPS EVERY-WHERE.

I WOULD BE THE FAN THAT WAFTS YOUR WHISPERS, YOUR SHADOWS THAT FOLLOW IN YOUR EVERY MOVE, THE CANDLES THAT SHINE UPON YOUR BEAUTEOUS FACE, THE BIRD THAT YOU FEED AND RETURN YOUR LOVE, THEN I WOULD LIVE. (OVER)

YET, WERE I ANYONE OF THESE THINGS,
I WOULD FEAR TO BE THE FORGOTTEN
DOVE, THE CASTAWAY FAN, THE SHADOWS
IN DARKNESS, THE CANDLES AT DAWN,
I LIVE IN VAIN.

(SHIENCHUNG)
TAO YUANMING

OBEY GOD'S WILL AND WAIT ON HEAVEN'S
PLEASURE. THY PURITY OF HEART, ALONE
DO TREASURE. LET BLOOM IN ORDER,
PEAR AND PEACH AND CHERRY. THE
MORROW LIES IN THE GOD'S LAP, WHY
WORRY?

TUNG CHUNGPENG

O COME WITH ME MY FRIEND AND WINE
SORROW. TO MATCH IT, THE MOON'S
GOLDEN LIQUID, BORROW. THEN, PASS
THE FRAGRANT CUP A TET-E-TETE OLD
FATHER HEAVEN WILL TAKE CARE OF THE
MORROW.

FU KUNGMON

IN TIMES OF PEACE, SPEAK AND ACT BY STERN PRINCIPLES, BUT, IN TIMES OF BAD GOVERNMENT, ACT BY STERN PRINCIPLES, BUT SPEAK VERY CAREFULLY.

CONFUCIUS

TRUE LITERATURE ALWAYS BRINGS OUT THAT ESSENTIAL CONFLICT OF HUMAN IMPERFECTIONS BECAUSE WE ARE NEITHER ANGELS, INCAPABLE OF EVIL, NOR BEASTS, INCAPABLE OF HIGHER OR NOBLER ASPIRATIONS. LOVE WILL ALWAYS BE WITH US AND SO WILL PAIN, MOMENTS OF JOY AND MOMENTS OF SUFFERING, BEAUTY AND UGLINESS, THE SINNER REPENTS AND THE GREAT MAN FALLS.

I THINK THE WORD UNDERSTANDING, IS A GREAT WORD. IT ASSERTS THE KINSHIP OF ALL MANKIND, BOTH, IN ITS LOVE OF TRUTH AND BEAUTY OF UNDERSTANDING.

LIN YUTANG

WHATEVER ONE READS, AT LEAST THE POSITION OF THE READER IS, ESSENTIALLY, THAT OF A SPECTATOR, AN OBSERVER OF LIFE

LIN YUTANG

THE ART OF STANDING

STAND STRAIGHT, BUT, DO NOT DO IT FOR LONG. OTHERWISE, ALL LEG MUSCLES WILL BECOME STIFF AND CIRCULATION WILL BE BLOCKED. LEAN ON SOMETHING. AN OLD PINE OR QUAINT ROCK, OR ON A BALCONY OR BAMBOO CANE. IT MAKES ONE LOOK LIKE ONE IS PAINTING. BUT, DO NOT LEAN ON A LADY. THE FOUNDATION IS NOT SOLID, THE ROOF MAY COME DOWN.

(THE ART OF LIVING)
LI LIWENG

EATING AND SEX FOLLOW INSTINCTS IN WHICH MEN AND ANIMALS ARE ALIKE. BEYOND THESE, IN THINGS OUTSIDE INSTINCTS THE TRUTH MUST BE LEARNED THROUGH SOME HARD THINKING

(KUEIYUYUAN CHUTAN)
SHU SHUEHOU

DO NOT WORRY THAT PEOPLE DO NOT KNOW YOU. WORRY THAT YOU MAY NOT BE WORTH KNOWING.

CONFUCIUS

ADMIT THAT YOU DO NOT KNOW WHAT YOU DO NOT KNOW. THAT IS KNOWLEDGE.

CONFUCIUS

STEAL A HOOK AND YOU ARE CALLED A CROOK, STEAL A KINGDOM, AND YOU ARE CALLED A DUKE.

CHUANGTSE

I AM BUSY SLEEPING THROUGHOUT THE WHOLE MORN, IF I LIVE TO SEVENTY FIVE AND THIRTY ARE GONE.

LI LIUENG

I REGARD THE HEAVEN AND EARTH AS MY COFFIN AND OUTER COFFIN, THE SUN AND MOON AS A PAIR OF JADE GIFTS, AND THE CONSTELLATIONS AS MY BURIAL JEWELS. AND THE WHOLE CREATION SHALL COME TO MY FUNERAL. WILL IT NOT BE A GRAND FUNERAL? WHAT MORE SHOULD I WANT?

CHUANGTSE

HE (THE ENLIGHTENED ONE) SIMPLY LOOKS UPON GOD AS HIS FATHER; IF HE LOVES HIM WITH WHAT IS BORN OF THE BODY, SHALL HE NOT LOVE HIM, ALSO, WITH THAT WHICH IS GREATER THAN THE BODY?

CHUANGTSE

PASSION HOLDS UP THE BOTTOM OF THE UNIVERSE, AND THE POET GIVES IT A NEW DRESS

YUMENGYING

STRICTLY SPEAKING, THERE SHOULD BE NO ORDER IN A BOOK OF THIS KIND WHICH IS DESIGNED FOR CASUAL DIPPING. MOST CHINESE ANTHOLOGIES OR SELECTIONS DO NOT BOTHER ABOUT ORDER. EACH PIECE SHOULD STAND BY ITSELF, TO BE DIPPED INTO WHEN THE READER FINDS A WORD OR A LINE ARRESTS HIS ATTENTION.

LIN YUTANG

WHEN A WRITER HAS A SENTIMENT IN HIS BREAST AND FEELS AN ITCH IN HIS FINGER, HE PUTS IT DOWN AND WHEN HE DOES IT BEAUTIFULLY ENOUGH FOR ALL READERS IN ALL AGES TO SHARE IT, IT BECOMES A CLASSIC. ARISTOTLE CALLS IT THE PLEASURE OF RECOGNITION. I WOULD PREFER TO CALL IT THE PLEASURE OF RELAXATION.

LIN YUTANG

THE WORLD HUSTLES
WHERE MONEY BECKONS
THE WORLD JOSTLES
WHERE PROFIT THICKENS

SZEMA CHIEN

WISDOM INFORMS THE MIND AND COOLS THE UNDERSTANDING, MAKING ONE SEE THINGS IN A BETTER PERSPECTIVE.

LIN YUTANG

SENTIMENT IS THE FRAGRANCE OF FLOWER, THE FLAVOR IN FOOD AND CHARM IN WOMAN.

LIN YUTANG

THE GREAT FLOOD
(UTNAPISHTIM to GILGAMESH)

THERE WAS A CITY CALLED SHURRUPAK
ON THE BANK OF THE EUPHRATES
IT WAS VERY OLD, AND SO MANY WERE THE GODS
WITHIN IT. THEY CONVERGED IN THEIR
COMPLEX HEARTS, ON THE IDEA OF CREATING
A GREAT FLOOD. THERE WAS ANU,
THEIR AGING AND WEAK MINDED FATHER
THE MILITARY ENLIL, HIS ADVISER
ISHTAR, THE SENSATION CRAVING ONE
AND ALL THE REST, EA, WHO WAS PRESENT
AT THEIR COUNCIL, CAME TO MY HOUSE
AND FRIGHTENED BY THE VIOLENT WINDS
THAT FILLED THE AIR, ECHOED ALL THAT
THEY WERE PLANNING AND HAD SAID
MAN OF SHURRUPAK, HE SAID, TEAR DOWN
YOUR HOUSE AND BUILD A SHIP. ABANDON
YOUR POSSESSIONS AND THE WORKS THAT
YOU FIND BEAUTIFUL AND CRAVE, AND SAVE
YOUR LIFE INSTEAD. INTO THE SHIP
BRING THE SEED OF ALL THE LIVING CREATURES
I WAS OVERAWED, PERPLEXED
AND FINALLY DOWNCAST, I AGREED TO DO
AS EA SAID, BUT PROTESTED WHAT SHALL
I SAY TO THE CITY THE PEOPLE THE LEADERS?
TELL THEM EA SAID YOU HAVE LEARNED THAT
ENLIL THE WAR GOD DESPISES YOU AND WILL
NOT GIVE YOU ACCESS TO THE CITY ANYMORE.
TELL THEM FOR THIS EA WILL BRING THE RAINS
THAT IS THE WAY GODS THINK
HE LAUGHED, HIS TONE OF SAVAGE IRONY
FRIGHTENED GILGAMESH, YET GAVE HIM
PLEASURE, BEING HIS FRIEND, THEY ONLY
KNOW HOW TO COMPETE OR ECHO. BUT,
WHO AM I TO TALK? HE SIGHED AS IF
DISGUSTED WITH HIMSELF, I DID AS HE
COMMANDED ME TO DO, I SPOKE TO THEM
AND SOME CAME OUT TO HELP ME BUILD THE
SHIP OF SEVEN STORIES, EACH WITH NINE

CHAMBERS, THE BOAT WAS CUBE IN SHAPE
AND SOUND IT HELD THE FOOD AND WINE
AND PRECIOUS MINERALS AND SEED OF
LIVING ANIMALS WE PUT IN IT. MY FAMILY
THEN MOVED INSIDE AND ALL WHO WANTED TO
BE WITH US THERE, THE GAME OF THE FIELD
THE GOATS OF THE STEPPE, THE CRAFTS-
MEN OF THE CITY CAME,A NAVIGATOR CAME
AND THEN EA ORDERED ME TO CLOSE THE DOOR.
THE TIME OF THE GREAT RAINS HAD COME.
O THERE WAS AMPLE WARNING, YES, MY FRIEND
BUT, IT WAS TERRIFYING, STILL. BUILDINGS
BLOWN BY THE WINDS FOR MILES LIKE DESERT
BRUSH, PEOPLE CLUNG TO BRANCHES OF TREES
UNTIL ROOTS GAVE WAY. NEW POSSESSIONS
NOW DEBRIS FLOATED ON THE WATER WITH
THEIR SPECIAL STERILE VACANCY.
THE RIVERBANKS FAILED TO HOLD THE WATER
BACK, EVEN THE GODS COWERED LIKE DOGS
AT WHAT THEY HAD DONE. ISHTAR CRIED OUT
LIKE A WOMAN AT THE HEIGHT OF LABOR, O
HOW COULD I HAVE WANTED TO DO THIS TO
MY PEOPLE! THEY WERE HERS, NOTICE.
EVEN HER SORROW WAS POSSESSIVE. HER
SPAWN THAT SHE HAD KILLED TOO SOON. OLD
GODS ARE TERRIBLE TO LOOK AT WHEN THEY
WEEP, ALL BLOATED LIKE SPOILED FISH. ONE
WONDERS IF THEY EVER UNDERSTAND THAT
THEY HAVE CAUSED THEIR GRIEF. WHEN THE
SEVENTH DAY CAME, THE FLOOD SUBSIDES
FROM ITS SLAUGHTER LIKE HAIR DRAWN SLOWLY
BACK FROM A TORMENTED FACE. I LOOKED
AT THE EARTH AND ALL WAS SILENCE.
BODIES LAY LIKE ALEWIVES, A TYPE OF FISH,
DEAD, AND IN THE CLAY, I FELL DOWN ON
THE SHIP'S DECK AND WEPT. WHY? WHY DID
THEY HAVE TO DIE? I COULD NOT UNDERSTAND.

I ASKED UNANSWERABLE QUESTIONS A CHILD ASKS WHEN A PARENT DIES FOR NOTHING.
ONLY SLOWLY DID I MAKE MYSELF BELIEVE OR HOPE THEY MIGHT ALL BE SWEPT UP IN THEIR FRAGMENTS, TOGETHER AND MADE WHOLE AGAIN BY SOME COMPASSIONATE HAND BUT MY HAND WAS TOO SMALL TO DO THE GATHERING. I HAVE ONLY KNOWN THIS FEELING SINCE WHEN I LOOK OUT ACROSS THE SEA OF DEATH, THIS PULL INSIDE AGAINST A LITTLENESS, MYSELF, WAITING FOR AN UPWARD GESTURE.
O THE DOVE, THE SWALLOW AND THE RAVEN FOUND THEIR LAND. THE PEOPLE LEFT THE SHIP, BUT, I FOR A LONG TIME COULD ONLY STAY INSIDE. I COULD NOT FACE THE DEATHS I KNEW WERE THERE.
THEN I RECEIVED ENLIL,
FOR EA HAD CHOSEN ME, THE WAR GOD TOUCHED MY FOREHEAD, HE BLESSED MY FAMILY AND SAID, BEFORE THIS YOU WERE JUST A MAN, BUT NOW, YOU AND YOUR WIFE SHALL LIVE IN THE DISTANCE AT THE RIVER' MOUTH, AT THE SOURCE. I ALLOWED MYSELF TO BE TAKEN FAR AWAY FROM ALL THAT I HAD SEEN. SOMETIMES, EVEN IN LOVE WE YEARN TO LEAVE MANKIND.
ONLY THE LONELINESS OF THE <u>ONLY</u> <u>ONE</u> WHO NEVER ACTS LIKE GODS IS BEARABLE.
I AM DOWN CAST BECAUSE OF WHAT I'VE SEEN NOT WHAT I STILL HAVE HOPE TO YEARN FOR LOST YOUTHS RESTORED TO LIFE.
LOST CHILDREN TO THEIR CRYING MOTHERS, LOST WIVES, LOST FRIENDS, LOST HOPES, LOST HOMES, I WANT TO BRING THESE BACK TO THEM. BUT, NOW THERE IS YOU.

WE MUST FIND SOMETHING FOR YOU.
HOW WILL YOU FIND ETERNAL LIFE?
TO BRING BACK TO YOUR FRIEND?
HE PONDERED BUSILY, AS IF IT WERE JUST
A MATTER OF GETTING DOWN TO WORK OR
MAKING PLANS FOR AN EXCURSION. THEN HE
RELAXED AS IF THERE WERE NO USE
IN THIS REFLECTION, I WOULD GRIEVE AT
ALL THAT MAY BEFALL YOU, STILL, IF I DID
NOT KNOW YOU MUST RETURN AND BURY YOUR
OWN LOSS AND BUILD YOUR WORLD ANEW WITH
YOUR OWN HANDS. IS ENVY YOU
FOR YOUR FREEDOM.
AS HE LISTENED, GILGAMESH FELT TIREDNESS
AGAIN COME OVER HIM, THE WORDS NOW SO
DISCOURAGING, THE PROMISE, SO REMOTE,
SO UNLIKE WHAT HE SOUGHT. HE LOOKED INTO
THE OLD MAN'S FACE AND IT SEEMED CHANGED,
AS IF THIS ONE HAD FOUGHT WITHIN
HIMSELF A BATTLE HE WOULD NEVER KNOW,
THAT STILL WENT ON.

(RETOLD BY HERBERT MASON)

YOU ARE ALIVE, BUT, I BELONG TO DEATH.

(ANTIGONE TO ISMENE)

AS A RAVENING FIRE BLAZES OVER A VAST
FOREST ON THE MOUNTAINS AND ITS LIGHT IS
SEEN AFAR, SO WHILE THEY MARCHED THE
SHEEN FROM THEIR FOREST OF BRONZE, SPEARS
WENT UP DAZZLING INTO HIGH HEAVEN

(HOMER, FROM THE 'ILIAD')

ON A QUIET NIGHT

I SAW THE MOONLIGHT BEFORE MY COUCH
AND WONDERED IF IT WERE NOT THE FROST
ON THE GROUND
I RAISED MY HEAD AND LOOKED OUT ON THE
MOUNTAIN MOON
I BOWED MY HEAD AND THOUGHT OF MY
FAR-AWAY-HOME.

Li bo

HARD IS THE JOURNEY

GOLD VESSELS OF FINE WINES
THOUSANDS A GALLON
JADE DISHES OF RARE MEATS
COSTING MORE THOUSANDS,
I LAY MY CHOPSTICKS DOWN,
NO MORE CAN BANQUET
AND DRAW MY SWORD AND STARE
WILDLY ABOUT ME
ICE BARS MY WAY TO CROSS
THE YELLOW RIVER
SNOWS FROM DARK SKIES TO CLIMB
THE Tai-hang MOUNTAINS
AT PEACE I DROP A HOOK
INTO A BROOKLET
AT ONCE I AM IN A BOAT
BUT, SAILING SUNWARD
HARD IS THE JOURNEY
HARD IS THE JOURNEY
SO MANY TURNINGS
AND NOW WHERE AM I?
SO WHEN A BREEZE BREAKS WAVES
BRINGING FAIR WEATHER
I SET A CLOUD FOR SAILS,
CROSS THE BLUE OCEANS!

Li Bo

AND WHEN THEY CAME TO THE BANKS OF THE SCAMANDER THOSE THOUSANDS DIED. AND WHY?
NO MAN HAD MOVED THEIR LANDMARKS
OR LAID SIEGE TO THEIR HIGH WALLED TOWNS
BUT, THOSE WHOM WAR TOOK NEVER SAW THEIR CHILDREN.
NO WIFE WITH GENTLE HANDS SHROUDED THEM FOR THEIR GRAVE.
THEY LIE IN A STRANGE LAND AND IN THEIR HOMES ARE SORROWS, TOO, THE VERY SAME. LONELY WOMEN WHO DIED, OLD MEN WHO WAITED FOR SONS THAT NEVER CAME NO SON LEFT TO THEM TO MAKE THE OFFERING AT THEIR GRAVES. THAT WAS THE GLORIOUS VICTORY THEY WON.

(EURIPIDES' THE TROJAN WOMEN)

I HEARD FROM A NEIGHBORING HOUSE, A VOICE AS OF A BOY OR GIRL, I KNOW NOT CHANTING AND OFT REPEATING, "TAKE UP AND READ, TAKE UP AND READ", SO I AROSE INTERPRETING IT TO BE NO OTHER THAN A COMMAND FROM GOD TO OPEN THE BOOK AND READ THE FIRST CHAPTER I SHOULD FIND.

(AUGUSTINE'S CONFESSION)

EVERY THING THAT IS RIGHT BEGS FOR SEPARATION FROM BRITAIN. THE AMERICANS HAVE BEEN KILLED SEEM TO SAY, "TIS TIME TO PART. ENGLAND AND AMERICA ARE LOCATED A GREAT DISTANCE APART. THAT IS ITSELF STRONG AND NATURAL PROOF THAT GOD NEVER EXPECTED ONE TO RULE OVER THE OTHER.

(THOMAS PAINE'S COMMON SENSE)

"COME ON, LET ME BUY YOU SOME BREAKFAST"
HOUSE OF SECRETS

"DID YOU JUST SHOOT AT ME WITH YOUR EYES CLOSED?" I, ROBOT

AN OUTLINE OF "POPE JOHN PAUL II : THE LIFE OF KAROL WOJTYLA by MIECZXSLAW MAKINSKI"

1. POLISH POPE 10-16-78

2. THE OCCUPATION

3. THE POPE'S MESSAGE 10-17-78

4. THE LIVING ROSARY

5. WHO IS THE POPE? 10-18-78

6. SECRET STUDIES

7. COLLEGIALITY 10-19-78

8. WAR AND PEACE

9. THE APOSTOLIC SEE 10-20-78

10. RECONSTRUCTION

11. FREEDOM OF SPEECH 10-21-78

12. KAROL'S EXPEDITIONS (LECTURES)

13. THE POPE'S INAUGURATION 10-22-78

14. BISHOP WOJTYLA
15. A POLISH POPE 10-23-78
16. THE COUNCIL
17. A CONVERSATION IN THE VATICAN 10-24-78
18. AT THE COUNCIL 9-14-64
19. THE MODERN AGE
20. METROPOLITAN OF CRACOW
21. THE POPE AT WORK
22. FOUNDATIONS OF RENEWAL
23. MRS. KOTLARCZYK REMEMBERS

ANGEL OF GOD, MY GUARDIAN DEAR,
TO WHOM HIS LOVE COMMITS ME
EVER THIS DAY AT MY SIDE
TO LIGHT AND GUARD, TO RULE
AND GUIDE AMEN

(DOMINICAN SISTERS OF HOPE)

NOVENA ROSE

O LITTLE THERESE OF THE CHILD, JESUS PLEASE PICK FOR ME A ROSE FROM THE HEAVENLY GARDENS AND SEND IT TO ME AS A MESSAGE OF LOVE. O LITTLE FLOWER OF JESUS, ASK GOD, TODAY TO GRANT THE FAVORS I NOW PLACE WITH CONFIDENCE IN YOUR HANDS. SAINT THERESE HELP ME TO ALWAYS BELIEVE AS YOU DID IN GOD'S GREAT LOVE FOR ME, SO THAT I MIGHT IMITATE YOUR LITTLE WAY EACH DAY. AMEN

(DOMINICAN SISTERS OF HOPE)

FOR NOW, WILL I BREAK HIS YOKE FROM OFF THEE AND WILL BURST THY BONDS IN SUNDER.

NAHUM 1: 13

BLESS US O LORD AND THESE YOUR GIFTS WHICH WE ARE ABOUT TO RECEIVE FROM YOUR BOUNTY THROUGH CHRIST OUR LORD. WE GIVE THANKS ALMIGHTY GOD FOR ALL YOUR BENEFITS, WHO LIVE AND REIGN WORLD WITHOUT END.

AMEN

(DOMINICAN SISTERS OF HOPE)

DEAR SISTER MARIA, IN OUR SADNESS

WHERE DO GREAT MEN GO, WHEN THEIR BURDEN OF GREATNESS IS LIFTED, NEVER, AGAIN, TO BE BORNE BY THEM? MEN GO WHERE MEN GO, OBVIOUSLY, BUT, THE GREATNESS, THEIR LIFE, JOINS THE OTHER GREATNESS THAT IS THE GREATER LIGHT OF HEAVEN. THE GREATER LIGHT THAT HAS SHONE FOR MILLIONS OF YEARS, RISING AND SETTING FOR ALL TO SEE. TO HAVE KNOWN ONE OR KNOWN OF ONE IN YOUR LIFETIME, IS SPECIAL, INDEED. OBVIOUSLY, POPE JOHN PAUL II HAS LEFT US, ONLY, TO RETURN TO US, FOREVER. THE WORLD IS A LITTLE LESS DARK FOR, YET, ANOTHER ONE, WHO HELPED LIFT THE VEIL OF DARKNESS, THAT IS OF THE WORLD. MAY HE SHINE WITH THE BRIGHTNESS THAT SHONE ON HIM IN HIS STAY ON EARTH. MAY SOMEONE BE TOUCHED BY THE EVER-LASTING LIGHT, THAT IS GOD.

YOUR FRIEND, EMD

POPE PAUL VI'S WAS THE EFFECT OF THAT OF THE GREAT POPE'S SENSE OF RESPONSIBILITY, FULL OF RESPECT AND BENEVOLENCE, FOR THE GENERAL GOOD OF NATIONS AND HIS UNDERSTANDING OF THE HIGH IDEALS OF PEACE AND DEVE-LOPMENT, WHICH INSPIRES THEM.

POPE JOHN PAUL II
(OF POPE PAUL VI)

JESUS, I WANT TO GROW IN HOLINESS AND IN LOVE FOR YOU. COME, OVER SHADOW ME WITH YOUR GRACE AND PRESENCE SO THAT I MAY GIVE TO OTHERS WHAT YOU HAVE GIVEN TO ME. LORD, HOW AWESOM AND MERCIFUL YOU ARE. TEACH ME HOW TO FAN INTO THE FLAME, THE GIFTS AND GRACE YOU HAVE GIVEN ME SO THAT I CAN BECOME AN INSTRUMENT OF YOUR POWER IN THIS WORLD. HEAVENLY FATHER, MOVE ME BY YOUR LOVE, TO LOVE YOU AND OTHERS WITH YOUR LOVE. HELP ME TO SEE MY LIFE, A FAITH AS A RELATIONSHIP, NOT JUST A DUTY. JESUS GIVE ME EARS OPEN TO HEAR YOUR VOICE. GIVE ME A HEART THAT TREASURES YOUR WORDS AND HUMBLY ACCEPTS EVERYTHING YOU SAY TO ME. SPEAK, LORD YOUR SERVANT IS LISTENING.

MEDITATIONS FROM THE WORD AMONG US

JOY IS THE KEYNOTE OF THE CHRISTIAN MESSAGE. FAITH IS OUR SOURCE OF JOY. WE BELIEVE IN A GOD WHO CREATED US SO THAT WE MIGHT ENJOY HUMAN HAPPINESS. WE ARE MEANT TO HAVE HUMAN JOYS, THE JOY OF LIVING, THE JOY OF LOVE AND FRIENDSHIP, THE JOY OF WORK WELL DONE. WE DISCOVER JOY WHEN WE DISCOVER TRUTH THE TRUTH ABOUT GOD OUR FATHER, THE TRUTH ABOUT JESUS OUR SAVIOUR, THE TRUTH ABOUT THE HOLY SPIRIT, WHO LIVES IN OUR HEARTS.

POPE JOHN PAUL II

GOD IS OUR FATHER

I BELIEVE THAT YOU ARE A FATHER TO ME AT EVERY MOMENT OF MY LIFE, AND THAT I AM YOUR CHILD. I BELIEVE THAT YOU LOVE ME WITH AN INFINITE LOVE. I BELIEVE THAT YOU ARE WATCHING OVER ME NIGHT AND DAY AND THAT NOT A HAIR FALLS FROM MY HEAD WITHOUT YOUR PERMISSION. I BELIEVE THAT IN YOUR INFINITE WISDOM, YOU KNOW BETTER THAN I , WHAT IS GOOD FOR ME. I BELIEVE THAT, IN YOUR INFINITE POWER, YOU CAN BRING GOOD, EVEN OUT OF EVIL. I BELIEVE THAT IN YOUR INFINITE GOODNESS, YOU MAKE EVERYTHING TO THE ADVANTAGE OF THOSE, WHO LOVE YOU. I BELIEVE, BUT, INCREASE IN ME FAITH, HOPE AND LOVE. DIVINE FATHER, CALL ALL MEN TO YOURSELF. LET ALL THE WORLD PROCLAIM YOUR FATHERLY GOODNESS AND YOUR DIVINE MERCY. DIVINE FATHER, SWEET HOPE OF OUR SOULS, MAY YOU BE KNOWN, HONORED AND LOVED BY ALL MEN.

MOTHER EUGENIA

MOTHER EUGENIA WAS BORN IN SAN GERVASIO d'ADDA, A SMALL TOWN IN THE PROVINCE OF BERGAMO, ITALY ON SEPTEMBER, 4, 1907, IN A FAMILY OF PEASANT BACKGROUND. SHE ENTERED THE CONGREGATION OF OUR LADY OF THE APOSTLES AT THE AGE OF TWENTY. SHE WAS ELECTED MOTHER GENERAL OF THE CONGREGATION AT THE AGE OF TWENTYFIVE,

IN TWELVE YEARS OF MISSIONARY ACTIVITY SHE OPENED OVER SEVENTY CENTERS, EACH WITH INFIRMARY, SCHOOL AND CHURCH IN THE REMOTEST SPOTS OF AFRICA, ASIA AND EUROPE. MOTHER EUGENIA DISCOVERED THE FIRST MEDICINE FOR THE CURE OF LEPROSY EXTRACTING IT FROM THE SEED OF A TROPICAL PLANT. FRANCE CONFERRED THE HIGHEST NATIONAL HONOR FOR SOCIAL WORK ON THE CONGREGATION OF OUR LADY OF THE APOSTLES, OF WHICH MOTHER EUGENIA WAS SUPERIOR GENERAL FROM 1935-1947.

MOTHER EUGENIA ELIZABETH RAVASIO DIED ON AUGUST 10, 1990.

FATHER ANDREA D' ACANIO OFM

GOD, OUR FATHER, YOU HAVE PROMISED YOUR KINGDOM TO THOSE WHO ARE WILLING TO BECOME LIKE LITTLE CHILDREN HELP US TO FOLLOW THE WAY OF THE LITTLE FLOWER WITH CONFIDENCE SO THAT BY HER PRAYERS, WE MAY COME TO KNOW YOUR ETERNAL GLORY. AMEN

(DOMINICAN SISTERS OF HOPE)

REMEMBER, O MOST COMPASSIONATE VIRGIN MARY, THAT NEVER WAS IT KNOWN THAT ANYONE WHO FLED TO YOUR PROTECTION IMPLORED YOUR ASSISTANCE OR SOUGHT YOUR INTERCESSION WAS LEFT UNAIDED. INSPIRED WITH THIS CONFIDENCE, WE FLY TO YOU, O VIRGIN OF VIRGINS, OUR MOTHER OF THE WORD INCARNATE, DESPISE NOT OUR PETITIONS, BUT, IN YOUR CLEMENCY, HEAR AND ANSWER THEM. IMMACULATE HEART OF MARY, PRAY FOR US.

(DOMINICAN SISTERS OF HOPE)

LOVE CAN ENDURE ALL
LOVE CAN BEAR ALL
IT CAN LIFT US UP SO HIGH
AND COMFORT US WHEN WE FALL
LOVE IS CLOSER THAN A FRIEND
AND DEARER THAN A MOTHER
LOVE CAN CREATE WONDERS
AND LOVE US LIKE NO OTHER.

EMD

"I KNEW I WOULDN'T WRITE THE GREAT AMERICAN NOVEL"

MEET JOE BLACK

"MY LIFE IS JUST REAL COMPLICATED"

BENNY AND JOON

"I NEVER TOLD YOU I LOVED YOU"

PLAY MISTY FOR ME

R

WORD NOOK 04-15-05
LANGUAGE RESEARCH SERVICE
P.O. BOX 281
SPRINGFIELD, MA 01102

DEAR EDITOR:

WHY DO PEOPLE USE THE CLICHES "I COULDN'T CARE LESS" AND "I COULD CARE LESS", SYNONOMOUSELY? "I COULD NOT" AMD "I COULD" ARE NOT SYNONOMOUS.

WHENEVER I USE "I COULDN'T CARE LESS" (I NEVER USE "I COULD CARE LESS"), IT IS MEANT THAT "I AM NOT THE LEAST BIT INTERESTED". THAT'S NOT THE SAME AS IF I SAID OR MEANT THAT I WAS INTERESTED.

I REALLY APPREACIATED YOUR ANSWER TO J.M., NORCROSS, GEORGIA, APRIL 2005, CONCERNING THE MOVIE FOLEY CREDITS.

SINCERELY YOURS,

ESTELLA DAVIS
MONROE, LOUISIANA

MERRIAM-WEBSTER, INC. AUGUST 24, 2005
47 FEDERAL STREET
P.O. BOX 281
SPRINGFIELD, MA 01102

MS. ESTELLA DAVIS
1617 ROGERS ST.
MONROE, LA 71201

DEAR ESTELLA:

YOUR LETTER ABOUT "COULDN'T CARE LESS" VERSUS "COULD CARE LESS" WAS GIVEN TO ME FOR A REPLY. PLEASE ACCEPT MY APOLOGIES FOR THE DELAY IN MY RESPONSE. I STARTED WRITING THIS LETTER BACK IN APRIL, BUT SET IT ASIDE TO CONCENTRATE ON ANOTHER PROJECT.

"COULD CARE LESS" HAS ATTRACTED ITS SHARE OF CRITISM OVER THE YEARS. THERE HAS BEEN MUCH ARGUMENT OVER WHY THE "COULD CARE LESS" FORM AROSE ("COULDN'T CARE LESS" IS THE OLDER PHRASE, AND IS THE ONLY FORM THAT IS USED IN GREAT BRITAIN.) NO PARTICULAR EXPLANATION HAS WON OUT OVER THE REST AS OF YET. ONE THING THAT LINGUISTS HAVE NOTICED THOUGH IS THAT THE INTONATION PATTERNS OF EACH PHRASE ARE DIFFERENT. IF YOU SAY "I COULDN'T CARE LESS" OUT LOUD, NEARLY EQUAL AMOUNTS OF STRESS FALL ON THE WORDS, COULDN'T AND CARE.

PERHAPS THE "I COULD CARE LESS" FORM AROSE IN AMERICAN SPEECH BECAUSE IT EMPHASIZES THE WORD, CARE. ACCORDING TO THIS TRAIN OF THOUGHT, THOSE PEOPLE WHO SAY "I COULD CARE LESS" WANT
(OVER)

EMPHASIZE CARE BECAUSE IT DRAWS ATTENTION TO THE FACT THAT THEY DON'T, IN FACT, CARE.

SOME PEOPLE DRAW A PARALLEL WITH THE INTONATIONS COMMONLY FOUND IN THE KIND OF SARCASTIC HUMOR THAT IS ASSOCIATED WITH THE IMMIGRANT JEWISH POPULATION OF NEW YORK CITY (I SHOULD BE SO LUCKY!"). THERE IS NO PROOF THAT "I COULD CARE LESS" WAS INFLUENCED BY THE YIDDISH-SPEAKING COMMUNITY, BUT, SOME FIND THIS SIMILARITY TO BE COMPELLING.

IF I MAY, I WOULD LIKE TO POINT OUT THAT THERE IS MORE THAN ONE WAY TO EXPRESS SARCASM. FOR INSTANCE, TAKE THE PHRASE "TELL ME ABOUT IT!, WHEN I SAY THAT, I REALLY MEAN "DON'T TELL ME ABOUT IT, BECAUSE I ALREADY KNOW EVERYTHING ABOUT IT." THE SORDS SAY ONE THING, BUT, MY TONE OF VOICE COMMUNICATES THE OPPOSITE MEANING. THE CONTRAST BETWEEN THE LITERAL MEANING OF THE WORDS AND THE TRUE MEANING OF THE UTTERANCE ENHANCES THE SARCASM. THIS I THINK, IS THE PROCESS AT WORK BEHIND UTTERANCES LIKE "FAT CHANCE!" AND "I COULD CARE LESS". WITH "I COULD CARE LESS," I THINK THE PERSON IS REALLY SAYING, "AS IF THERE WERE SOMETHING IN THE WORLD THAT I COULD CARE LESS ABOUT."

ON THE OTHER HAND, WITH "I COULDN'T CARE LESS," MEANING, AS YOU SAID, "I AM

(OVER)

NOT THE LEAST BIT INTERESTED," THE MEANING, ALONE COMMUNICATES THE INTENDED MESSAGE OF CONTEMPT.

I AM PUZZLED WHEN PEOPLE APPLY LOGIC TO LANGUAGE AND INSIST THAT, BECAUSE THE LITERAL MEANING DOESN'T MATCH UP WITH THE INTENDED MEANING, "I COULD CARE LESS" MUST BE WRONG. FIRST OF ALL, SO MUCH OF LANGUAGE IS NOT LOGICAL. APPLYING LOGIC TO SOME THING THAT DOESN'T BEHAVE ACCORDING TO THE RULES OF LOGIC CAN ONLY BE A FRUITLESS EXERCISE, I THINK. SECOND, LANGUAGE ISN'T INTERPRETED IN A VACUUM. THE LITERAL MEANING OF WORDS ISN'T THE ONLY THING THAT MATTERS IN A CONVERsation; TONE AND VOICE, BODY LANGUAGE AND SHARED KNOWLEDGE OF THE CONTEXT ARE ALSO TAKEN INTO ACCOUNT.

THE BEST OBJECTION TO "I COULD CARE LESS," IN MY OPINION, IS THAT IT'S A SENTENCE THAT WORKS MUCH BETTER IN SPEECH THAN IN WRITING. BUT, SAYING "IT'S BEST NOT TO USE 'I COULD CARE LESS' IN YOUR WRITING, SINCE IT COULD CONFUSE YOUR READERS IF THEY DON'T REALIZE THAT THEY SHOULDN'T TAKE IT LITERALLY" IS DIFFERENT FROM CONDEMNING "I COULD CARE LESS" OUTRIGHT OR CONTENDING THAT "I COULD CARE LESS" CAN ONLY MEAN THE OPPOSITE OF "I COULDN'T CARE LESS."

YOU MAY BE GLAD TO KNOW THAT MANY

OVER)

COMMENTATORS ON USAGE PREFER "I COULDN'T CARE LESS" BECAUSE IT'S UNAMBIGUOUS, "I COULDN'T CARE LESS" IS MORE COMMON IN WRITING THAN "I COULD CARE LESS," SINCE, IT'S DIFFICULT TO EXPRESS SARCASM USING THE WRITTEN WORD.

I HOPE I HAVE EXPLAINED TO YOUR SATISFACTION, WHY MANY PEOPLE USE "I COULD CARE LESS." THANK YOU, AGAIN, FOR YOUR PATIENCE.

SINCERELY,

JUDY YEH
ASSISTANT EDITOR

JY/elj

Share your opinion

Mail to
P.O. Box 1502,
Monroe, La. 71210

Fax to
(318) 362-0273

E-mail to
letters@thenewsstar.co

■ Include name, address and day phone number with letters. We may edit letters for accuracy, clarity and length. Limit to 250 words. Writers are limited to one letter per month.

■ Letters or columns may be published in electronic or other forms. We prefer letters that address current topics. No personal attacks. Letters without a return address will not be opened.

City has a bad visual image

As I was driving down U.S. 165 North recently, I noticed that the grass was about 3 feet high. It took the beautification department three weeks to pick up a huge pile of tree limbs in my front yard.

The city wants to raise the sales tax again, making Monroe one of the highest taxed cities in Louisiana. I could go on and on about things such as the high crime rate and low literacy and poor city administration, but I don't think it takes a genius to figure out why no company wants to relocate to this area. It makes me very sad, but I think that this city is in a downward spiral, and it will take a miracle to save it.

Clint Guillory
Monroe

These writings unmistakably reveal the Christian philosophy of life, government and education the founding fathers were trying to establish for the nation they were attempting to build.

Unfortunately historical revisionist, liberal secularist and judicial activist judges have censored our history and removed many of our right which "nature's God entitles them." Noah Webster's First Edition Dictionary would not even be allowed in our school libraries. Our pre-founding and early nation's basic school textbook is basically banned. Early text that taught people to read, spell, teach moral advice and ethics would not be permitted as teaching tools today.

Could we find 56 leaders who would "mutually pledge to each other our lives, our fortunes, and our sacred honor" for such a cause today. Leaders, no, but thanks to all our men and women in Iraq.

Byrd Minter
Monroe

Presidents are focus of attention

It's not likely that we have very much to comment about at this time without attention on our former or current presidential affairs. Reagan's death, Clinton's book and Bush's historical intervention in the Middle East crisis makes for foremost attention, even to those who don't consider modern political issues interesting.

I am sure Reagan will be remembered as the beloved president the way John was remembered as the beloved disciple in our Lord's day. Bush will surely be considered for his bravery in his involvement in the Middle East, with so much admitted craziness and actual insanity associated the war and its leaders.

Even if Clinton does not have the most experienced presidential library in history, he will be remembered as having the most humble first lady of modern times at his side during his troublesome terms as president. Had he had a lady with such attributes as "cocky" as with Jackie Kennedy, unintelligent as Rosalyn Carter or alcoholic as with Betty Ford, his circumstances would have been very different.

I am sincerely hoping Clinton never lacks understanding of how blessed he is to have had Virginia before him, Hillary beside him and Chelsea ahead of him.

Estella Davis
Monroe

THEY TOOK THE BEST YEARS OF MY LIFE. THEY ABUSED ME, PHYSICALLY AND MENTALLY. I DIDN'T GET TO SEE MY CHILDREN GROW UP. I HATED THEM. THEN I THOUGHT TO MYSELF. THEY HAVE HAD ME FOR TWENTY-SEVEN YEARS. IF I KEEP ON HATING THEM THEY WILL STILL HAVE ME. SO I FORGAVE THEM, SO I COULD BE FREE.

SOUTH AFRICAN, NELSON MANDELLA OF HIS ACCUSERS AND HIS TWENTY-SEVEN YEARS IN PRISON AT ROBBEN ISLAND.

BENJAMIN O. DAVIS, JR. MADE HISTORY FOR HIMSELF AND HIS COUNTRY WHEN, WHILE IN THE AIR FORCE, HE BECAME THE FIRST BLACK TO BECOME A GENERAL IN 1954. HIS FATHER BENJAMIN O. DAVIS, SR. HAD, ALREADY BECAME A GENERAL IN THE ARMY IN 1940.

AARP
LOOKING BACK

LADIES AND GENTLEMEN, ISN'T IT A WONDERFUL THING THAT PEOPLE CAN SPEAK THEIR MINDS IN OUR DEMOCRACY? IN BAGHDAD, THEY, TOO, WILL BE ABLE TO SPEAK THEIR MINDS. WHAT A WONDERFUL THING.

SEC. OF STATE CONDOLEEZZA RICE, PERFORMING SWEETLY AT THE PRESTIGIOUS SAN FRANCISCO COMMONWEALTH CLUB.

DIFFERING OPINIONS

I CONSIDER SLAVERY AN EVIL AND AM FOR CONFINING IT WITHIN AS SMALL A COMPASS, AS POSSIBLE.

SEN. JOHN BRENKENRIDGE
IN OPPOSITION TO
SLAVERY IN THE NEWLY
FORMED LOUISIANA AND
IT'S TERRITORIES.

WITHOUT THE AID OF SLAVES, NEITHER COFFEE NOR COTTON CAN BE RAISED. SLAVERY MUST BE ADMITTED INTO THE TERRITORY.

SEN. JAMES JACKSON
IN FAVOR OF ADMITTING
SLAVERY INTO THE NEW
LOUISIANA TERRITORY.

DEVINE PROVIDENCE OR MANIFEST DESTINY?

RESTLESS ACQUISITIVENESS
ENDLESS EXPANSION
ABSTRACT BOUNDARIES
REPUBLICAN VALUES
DEMOCRATIC IDEALS.

AMERICA IS BLESSED WITH THE SPIRITUAL AND PHYSICAL RESOURCES TO BECOME SELF-RELIANT.

FLEUR de LIS VS,
OLD GLORY.
THE TREATY OF PARIS
1777.

R

"WHERE ARE THE PAPER TOWELS?"

WHEN A MAN LOVES A WOMAN

"I DON'T KNOW HOW TO PLAY POKER"

FRIED GREEN TOMATOES

"ALL'S WELL THAT ENDS WELL"

FREAKY FRIDAY

"WHERE DO YOU PEOPLE COME FROM?

FIRST BLOOD

THERE'S ALWAYS A RAINBOW AFTER THE STORM.

NEW PROJECT

EVERY COUNTRY NEEDS TO PUT UP A UNITED FRONT AGAINST TERRORISM.

SEC. OF STATE
CONDOLEZZA RICE

WE CANNOT HELP, BUT, MOVE CLOSER TO GOD.

RUSSELL SIMMONS
GODFATHER OF HIP-HOP MMM 2005

WE MUST START, NOW, REDEEMING THE TIME. BLACK FOLKS HAVE ALWAYS BEEN THE CONSCIOUS OF THIS COUNTRY. WE ARE CALLED UPON, YET, AGAIN, TO BEAR THE BURDEN WE HAVE ALWAYS BORNE. AMERICA NEEDS LEADERSHIP WITH COURAGE AND CONVICTION TO DO WHAT WE HAVE TO DO.

TAVIS SMILEY
MMM 2005

GOD UNITES US IN SPIRIT. WHAT GOD JOINS TOGETHER, LET NO MAN PUT ASSUNDER.

EMD

YOU CANNOT LEAD THE PEOPLE, IF YOU DON'T LOVE THE PEOPLE. WE CANNOT SAVE THE PEOPLE IS WE DON'T SERVE THE PEOPLE.

CORNEL WEST
MMM 2005

WE ARE HERE TO REBUILD, REPAIR AND TO RECONSTRUCT OUR COMMUNITIES AND OUR NATIONS. WE ARE HERE IN THE SAME SPIRIT AS THAT OF MARCUS GARVEY.

REV, WILLIE WILSON
EXE. DIR. MILLION
MORE MOVEMENT 2005

WE THANK GOD FOR THIS BEAUTIFUL DAY, THE TENTH ANNIVERSARY OF THE MILLION MAN MARCH 1995.

REV. MARY WILSON
UNION TEMPLE B.C.
CO-PASTOR MMM 2005

THIS IS THE DAY THAT THE LORD HAS MADE. WE WILL BE GLAD AND REJOICE IN IT. WE HAVE COME TOGETHER AS A TAPESTRY OF UNITY; ORGANIZATIONS REPRESENTING A BROAD SPECTRUM OF PEOPLE.

DR. JULIANNE MALVEAUX
CEO LAST WORD PROD.
MMM 2005

TEN YEARS LATER, WE ARE, STILL STANDING. WE ARE FIGHTING IN IRAQ, WHEN WE DON'T HAVE DEMOCRACY IN THE DISTRICT OF COLUMBIA. BUT WE ARE STILL STANDING.

MARION BARRY
FORMER MAYOR (DC)
MMM 2005

WE ARE TO REPAIR, REBUILD, FIND A WAY TO BE A PART OF SOMETHING BIGGER THAN OURSELVES.

CORA MASTERS-BARRY
MMM 2005

WE ARE HERE TO UNDERSTAND WHAT FOLLOWING UP ON COMMITTMENTS MEAN. WE ARE HERE TO AGGITATE, ENCOURAGE AND DO WHAT IS NESCESSARY TO MAKE IT HAPPEN. HURRICANE KATRINA, DRAMATICALLY, HELPED THE FOCUS OF THE CONGRESSIONAL BLACK CAUCUS.

CONG. MEL WATT
(D) NORTH CAROLINA
MMM 2005

WE ARE TO MOVE OUR DREAMS, HOPES AND ASPIRATIONS A STEP CLOSER TO REALITY. WE ARE TO ORGANIZE AND STRATERGISE AND TO DO THE WILL OF THE PEOPLE.

REP. DANNY DAVIS
(D) ILLIINOIS
MMM 2005

REDEMPTION SONGS, SONGS OF REDEMPTION ARE ALL I'VE EVER HAD.

RECORDING
BOB MARLEY
MMM 2005

TODAY, AS FAR AS MY EYES CAN SEE, I SEE BEAUTIFUL PEOPLE OF ALL COLORS. THE HOPES THAT UNITE US ARE GREATER THAN THE FEARS THAT DIVIDE US.

MARC MORIAL
NAT. URBAN LEAGUE
PRES. & CEO
MMM 2005

THE MOST IMPORTANT TRAFFIC SIGN YOU WILL FIND ON THE HIGHWAY OF LIFE IS A STOP SIGN, A RED SIGNAL, A FLASHING LIGHT. WHEN LEARNING TO DRIVE AN AUTOMOBILE, OF ALL THE GIZMOS YOU WILL BE USING, THE BRAKE OR THE STOP PEDAL WILL PROVE TO BE THE MOST IMPORTANT. THIS IS BECAUSE WE MUST ACQUIRE A SENSE OF FORGIVENESS TO GET ANYWHERE IN LIFE. AND FOREGIVENESS IS NOT POSSIBLE WITHOUT REPENTENCE AND REPENTENCE IS NOT POSSIBLE WITHOUT COMING TO A FULL STOP. NOT JUST A CAUTION, WAIT, SLOW-DOWN OR YEILD, BUT, A COMPLETE STOP. WE FIND THAT WHEN WE DO THIS IN ANY AREA OF OUR LIVES, A NEW BEGINNING IS REALIZED AND AS WITH ALL NEWNESS OR BEGINNINGS, THEREIN LIES HOPE. HOPE FOR THE FUTURE, HOPE FOR THE REST OF THE DAY,HOPE FOR THE REST OF THE JOURNEY.

EMD

EXPERIENCE IS NOT WHAT HAPPENS TO YOU, IT IS WHAT YOU DO WITH WHAT HAPPENS TO YOU.

ALDOUS HUXLEY

YOU CANNOT CREATE EXPERIENCE, YOU MUST UNDERGO IT.

ALBERT CAMUS

BY FAR, THE BEST PROOF IS EXPERIENCE.

SIR FRANCIS BACON

REMEMBERING THE CLASS OF 1976
CONTRA COSTA COLLEGE
SAN PABLO, CALIFORNIA
EMD

UNITY BEGINS WITH PRAISE. PRAISE IS WHAT I DO , PRAISE IS WHAT I AM. BEGIN TO BLESS GOD. I WILL PRAISE HIM WHILE I CAN.

CHICANO GLORY
MINISTRIES
MMM 2005

OUR MINDS BEGIN TO END, THE DAY WE BECOME SILENT.

MARTIN LUTHER KING

IT IS ESSENTIAL THAT WE SPEAK OUT ON INJUSTICE HERE AND INJUSTICE EVERYWHERE.

BILL FLETCHER
MMM 2005

WE ARE ONE. ARE WE READY TO WALK IN FAITH TODAY? ARE WE READY TO LOVE ONE ANOTHER AS WE LOVE OURSELVES. ARE WE READY TO UNITE? THIS DAY OUGHT TO BE A DAY OF COMMITTMENT. THIS IS NOT A MARCH, THIS IS A MOVEMENT. WE ARE ONE.

BARBARA WILLIAMS-
SKINNER PROGRAM
COMMITTEE CHAIR.
MMM 2005

NO MATTER WHAT HAPPENS, HE'S GOT THE WHOLE WORLD IN HIS HANDS.

BRENDA JACKSON
BERLIN OPERA HOUSE
MMM 2005

FAILURE IS A WORD I DO NOT ACCEPT.

JOHN H. JOHNSON

FREEDOM FOR EVERYBODY OR FREEDOM FOR NOBODY.

RON DANIELS
MMM 2005

WE MAY HAVE COME IN DIFFERENT BOATS, BUT, WE ARE, NOW, ALL IN THE SAME SHIP. SELDOM DO WE DO WHAT WE WANT, BUT, WE ALWAYS DO WHAT WE HAVE TO DO. NO ONE WILL DO FOR YOU, WHAT YOU CAN DO FOR YOURSELF.

DR. DOROTHY HEIGHT
MMM 2005

YOU HAVE OUR DEEPEST FEELINGS OF BROTHERHOOD.

RICARDO ALACORN
CUBAN NATIONAL
ASSEMBLY MMM 2005

WE STAND IN SOLIDARITY, AS SISTERS AND BROTHERS. THE MARCH MUST BEGIN IN OUR HEARTS. WE MUST REACH BEYOND THE MOVEMENT. LIKE GHANDI, OUR LIFE MUST BE OUR MESSAGE.

P.J. PATTERSON
JAMAICAN PRIME
MINISTER MMM 2005

THE PEOPLE OF HAITI NEED YOU. GIVE HAITIANS THEIR RIGHT OF DUE PROCESS. BRING OUR VOICES TOGETHER, HAITIANS ARE BEING HELD AS PRISONERS OF CONSCIOUS BY OTHER PEOPLE BEING HELD IN BONDAGE.

MOLLIENE BASTILLE
NATION OF HAITI

MILLIONS MORE MOVEMENT

CLEO MANAGO
BLACK MEN'S EXCHANGE FOUNDATION
MMM 2005

HASHIM NZINGA
NEW BLACK PANTHER PARTY
MMM 2005

RUKIA LUMUMBA
MALCOM X GRASS ROOTS COALITION
MMM 2005

EFIA NWGA NWANGAZA
MMM 2005

JITU WEUSI
NATIONAL BLACK UNITED FRONT
MMM 2005

MACHEO SHABAKA
AAPRP
MMM 2005
RAY WINBUSH
GLOBAL AFRICAN CONGRESS
MMM 2005

HATIANS ARE BEING HELD PRISONERS BY BLACKS, WHO ARE BEING HELD IN BONDAGE BY WHITES, WHO ARE VICTIMS OF GLOBAL SABOTAGE. BY SABOTAGE, WE MEAN THAT PRESIDENT GEORGE WALKER BUSH IS BEING ACCUSED OF NOT HEEDING THE CALL OF GLOBAL WARNING AND, THUS, WAS SLOW IN RESPONDING TO THE CALL FOR HELP BY VICTIMS OF HURRICANE KATRINA.

(OPINION)
EMD

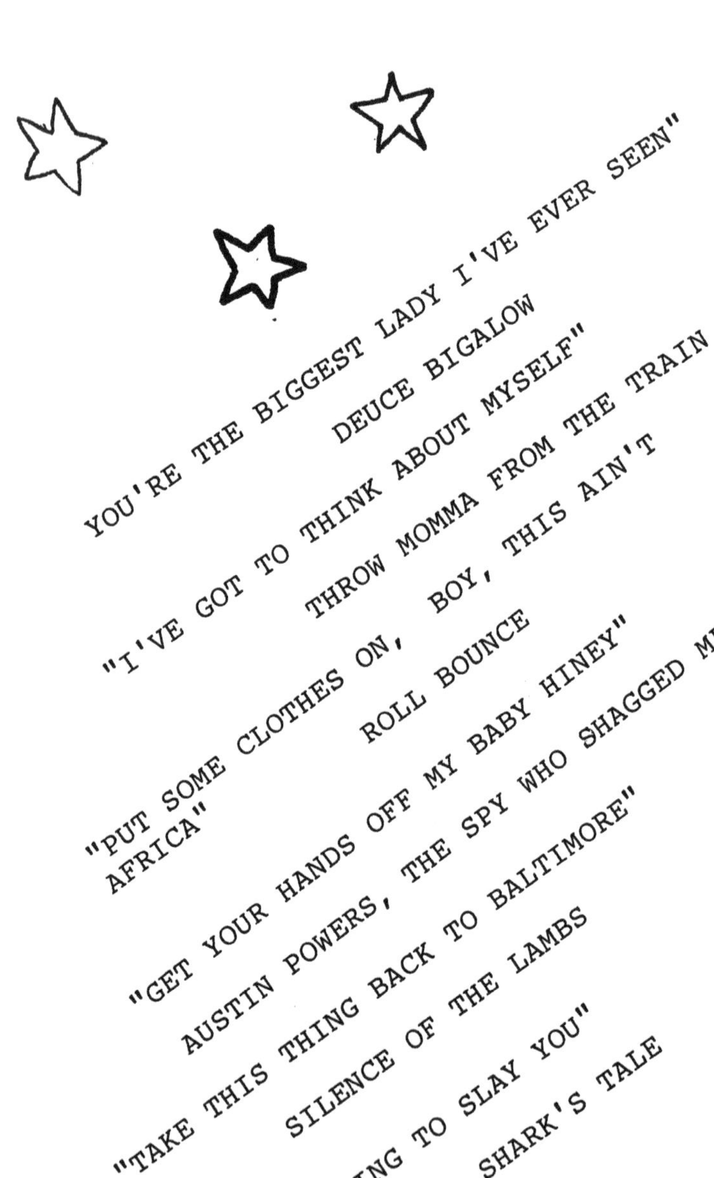
YOU'RE THE BIGGEST LADY I'VE EVER SEEN"
DEUCE BIGALOW
"I'VE GOT TO THINK ABOUT MYSELF"
THROW MOMMA FROM THE TRAIN
"PUT SOME CLOTHES ON, BOY, THIS AIN'T
AFRICA"
ROLL BOUNCE
"GET YOUR HANDS OFF MY BABY HINEY"
AUSTIN POWERS, THE SPY WHO SHAGGED ME
"TAKE THIS THING BACK TO BALTIMORE"
SILENCE OF THE LAMBS
AND HE'S GOING TO SLAY YOU"
A SHARK'S TALE

THE DIFFERENCE IN THE 'MARCH AND THE MOVEMENT'

WHEN I WAS IN HIGH SCHOOL, I RECALL A DAY WHEN MY ENGLISH TEACHER WAS GIVING SEMESTER OR QUARTERLY EXAMS. ENGLISH WAS ALWAYS A VERY GOOD STUDY FOR ME AND I APPROACHED IT WITH VERY LITTLE EFFORT.

THIS DAY, I WAS SEATED IN BACK OF THE CLASSROOM DOING MY TEST PAPER, (YOU COULD THROW SPITBALLS OR CHEW BUBBLE-GUM IF YOU SAT IN BACK AND TEACHER DID NOT CATCH YOU), WHICH WAS VARIETY, INCLUDING UNDERLINING THE SUBJECT, VERB AND OBJECT IN SEVERAL SENTENCES. I WAS BUSY UNDERLINING SUBJECT, VERB AND OBJECTS, WHEN I GOT TO THE LAST SENTENCE ON A PAGE BEFORE I WAS READY TO HAND IN MY PAPER. THE SENTENCE READ, "CONJUGATE THE VERB, TO BE. I IMMEDIATELY UNDERLINED THE 'UNDERSTOOD' SUBJECT, 'YOU', THE VERB, 'CONJUGATE' AND THE OBJECT, 'VERB'. BOY, THAT WAS EASY.

AT THAT TIME, I LOOKED AROUND AND SAW EVERYBODY, ELSE, BUSY, DOING SOMETHING ON THEIR PAPER. SO, FINALLY, I LOOKED AT MY PAPERS AGAIN AND REALIZED TEACHER WANTED ME CONJUGATE THE VERB 'TO BE' AND NOT TO UNDERLINE THE SUBJECT, VERB AND OBJECT, AS SOME OF THE PREVIOUS SENTENCES WERE DONE.

ACTUALLY, CONJUGATING THE VERB, 'TO BE', AS ANY ENGLISH STUDENT WILL KNOW, TAKES

(OVER)

(CON'D)

MUCH LONGER THAN UNDERLINING THREE WORDS IN A SENTENCE. SO, I GOT BUSY TO START CONJUGATING AT THE LAST MOMENT, AS ALL THE OTHER STUDENTS WERE ALREADY HANDING IN THEIR PAPERS. THIS WAS ONE TEST I ALWAYS REMEMBERED BECAUSE I, ALMOST, DIDN'T ANSWER THAT QUESTION, WHICH WAS OF MORE VALUE THAN THE UNDERLINED SENTENCES WERE AND COULD HAVE BEEN THE DIFFERENCE IN A GOOD GRADE AND A FAILING ONE.

FROM THAT TIME ON, I WAS CAREFUL TO REALLY ANALYZE THE DIRECTIONS ON THE PAPER. THE ENGLISH TEACHER WAS ONE KNOWN BY ALL HER STUDENTS AS THE WOMAN WHO NEVER SMILED. AND SHE, ALMOST, NEVER LET A STUDENT CATCH HER WITH A SMILE ON HER FACE. I HAD SEEN HER WITH A SMILE ON HER FACE, FOR I CHECKED A LOT OF PAPERS FOR HER AND TOOK NAMES OF KIDS WHO HABITUALLY, 'CUT-UP' IN CLASS. SO, I KNEW SHE COULD SMILE IF SHE WANTED. BUT, THIS WOULD HAVE BEEN NO LAUGHING MATTER FOR HER IF I HAD FAILED TO CONJUGATE THE VERB, 'TO BE'.

THIS, PARTICULAR, ABRAHAM LINCOLN-LOOKING WOMAN TEACHER WAS EVERY BIT AS STERN AS ANY OF THE MALE TEACHERS. SHE KEPT, BOTH, SWITHCHES FOR GIRLS-AND BELTS FOR BOYS ON HER DESK IN ADDITION TO EVERYTHING ELSE SHE NEEDED TO COMMIT 'CORPORAL PUNISHMENT' IN THE CLASSROOM.

(OVER)

(CON'D)

I USED TO SPEND FIFTEEN MINUTES IN FRONT OF THE CLASS, TRYING TO HOLD OUT MY HANDS FOR HER TO SWITCH, FINALLY, SHE WOULD, JUST SWITCH MY LEGS AND GET IT OVER. EVERYBODY WAS A VICTIM IN HER CLASS. NO ONE WAS EXEMPT. I WAS VERY WELL BEHAVED, BUT, IF YOUR NAME GOT ON THE LIST, SHE JUST WENT DOWN THE LIST.

DOWN SOUTH SCHOOLS DIDN'T MISS A THING. THEY PUT IT ALL IN AND CALLED IT LEARNING, AS WELL AS EDUCATION. YOU KNEW THAT THE DESK, PENCIL, PAPER AND YOU CONSTITUTED THE FOUR THINGS YOU WOULD COME IN CONTACT WITH FOR THE REST OF YOUR LIFE. THE TREE WAS HERALD LIKE NO PLACE ELSE AS SOMETHING ALMIGHTY. AND THAT WAS BEFORE I EVER WENT TO CALIFORNIA TO SEE THE OLDEST AND TALLEST LIVING THINGS, THE REDWOODS.

EMD

GIVE YOU UP

WE DIDN'T WANT TO GIVE YOU UP,
WE'LL MISS THAT SMILE ON YOUR FACE
BUT, COMFORTED ARE WE BY THIS THOUGHT
IN HEAVEN, YOU WILL TAKE YOUR PLACE
WE DIDN'T WANT TO GIVE YOU UP
YOUR PASSING, THOUGH, DOES MAKE US SAD
BUT, STILL, WE'RE CONSOLED WITH THIS
THOUGHT, IN HEAVEN YOU WILL BE GLAD
WE DIDN'T WANT TO GIVE YOU UP
YET, WE KNOW YOU'VE GONE TO REST, SO
COMFORTED ARE WE BY THIS THOUGHT
TO BE IN HEAVEN IS THE BEST,

A FUNERAL THOUGHT

THE OLD MAN AND THE RIVER

ONCE UPON A TIME, THERE WAS AN OLD MAN. THE OLD MAN HAD SEVERAL CHILDREN AND GRANDCHILDREN. THE OLD MAN DID NOT HAVE A CAREER, LIKE MOST PEOPLE DO, BUT, HE DID WORK AND HE DID HAVE A JOB. HE WOULD RISE EARLY EACH DAY AT DAWN AND LEAVE FOR THE RIVERBANK, TO SPEND THE DAY DRAWING THE FISH TO HIM. HE BECAME SUCH A GOOD FISHERMAN, HE COULD PREDICT, ACCURATELY, HOW MANY FISH HE WOULD CATCH BY DUSK, WHEN HE WOULD BEGIN TO HEAD BACK HOME.

HE WALKED THE SEVERAL MILES DAILY TO AND FROM THE RIVERBANK AND THIS EXERCISE KEPT HIM SO FIT, HE NEVER HAD ANY FAT, TO BE SEEN, ON HIS BODY. HE BELIEVED THAT TOO MUCH LYING DOWN WAS NOT GOOD FOR ONE'S HEART AND LUNGS AND SLEPT PART OF THE NIGHT IN A SITTING-UP POSITION.

HE BELIEVED IN A LOT OF HOMEMADE OR FAMILIAR REMEDIES AND HAD VERY LITTLE USE FOR STORE BOUGHT MEDICINE. HE BELIEVED MAN WAS MADE TO WALK, BUT, HE HAD ONE SON THAT LIVED AND BREATHED AUTOMOBILES AND ONE THAT RODE ONLY BICYCLES.

WHENEVER HE WOULD BRING HIS CATCH OF FISH HOME, SOME OF HIS CHILDREN OR GRANDCHILDREN WOULD ALWAYS BE AROUND TO SCALE THE VERY LARGE AND VERY SMALL RIVER GROWN FISH.

(OVER)

ASK ANY GIRL ABOUT FISH SCALES AND SHE WILL TELL YOU IT IS SOMETHING SHE WOULD RATHER NOT EVER HAVE TO DO. ONE DAY THE OLD MAN BROUGHT HOME A VERY LARGE CAT FISH. I AM ALLERGIC TO ANIMAL FUR AND CAN'T STAND CATS AND ALWAYS THOUGHT THE CAT HAD SOMETHING TO DO WITH THE CATFISH. HE TOLD ME TO HEAT A POT OF WATER ON THE STOVE. HE SAID THAT THE WATER SHOULD BE HOT ENOUGH TO REMOVE THE SKIN OFF THE FISH, BUT, NOT SO HOT THAT THE FLESH WOULD BE TOUGHENED AND UNFIT TO EAT.

LATER, WHEN I GREW UP, I UNDERSTOOD MY GRANDFATHER'S LIFESTYLE AS WELL AS THE MORAL OF SOME OF THE ASPECTS OF HIS ECCENTRIC WAY OF LIVING. EVEN THOUGH HE CHOSE FISHING, AS A WAY OF PROVISIONS, HE ALLOWED FOR VERY DIFFERENT CHOICES THAT HIS SONS WOULD MAKE FOR THEMSELVES. THE CATFISH MORAL WAS SIMILAR TO LIFE CHOICES. THE VERY THING THAT YOU NEED SOMETIMES, CAN BE THE THING TO HARM YOU IF ABUSED OR MISUSED. THE HOT WATER WOULD REMOVE THE SKIN FROM THE FISH TO READY THE FISH FOR COOKING AND EATING, BUT, IF THE WATER IS TOO HOT, THE FISH WOULD BE RUINED AND NOT FIT TO EAT AND THE DAY WASTED. THE END

EMD

A HIGH SCHOOL FAREWELL

FAREWELL TO DEAR OLD CARROLL, WHERE WE'VE LIVED AND LEARNED TO LOVE. THE HOUR, FOR WHICH WE WAITED, LONG, IS SWIFTLY DRAWING NEAR. TO THE DEAR OLD HALLS OF CARROLL, EVERY VOICE NOW BID FAREWELL. BUT, THINK OF US FROM YEAR TO YEAR, NOT LOST, BUT, GONE BEFORE. FOR ALL OUR WORK WELLDONE, WE'VE CROSSED THE RUGGED ROAD. WE KNOW NOT WHAT THE FUTURE HAS IN STORE, BUT AS WE SADLY START OUR JOURNEYS FAR APART, A PART OF EVERY HEART WILL LINGER HERE. FOR WE HATE TO LEAVE THEE CARROLL. FAREWELL OLD FRIENDS SO DEAR. THE HOUR FOR WHICH WE'VE WAITED LONG IS SWIFTLY DRAWING NEAR. WE HAVE LOVED OUR DEAREST TEACHERS AND OUR PRINCIPAL SO TRUE, WHO HAVE DONE THEIR BEST TO GUIDE US THE WAY WE SHOULD GO. WE SHALL EVER LOVE YOU AND REMEMBER THROUGH THE YEARS, THE DAYS WE'VE SPENT AT CARROLL HIGH. SO NOW, WE SAY GOOD BYE. ONE DAY, A HUSH WILL FALL. THE FOOTSTEPS OF US, ALL WILL ECHO DOWN THE HALL AND EVERY HEART WILL LINGER HERE, TO THE FAMOUS HALL OF CARROLL AND TO OUR FRIENDS, SO DEAR. THE TIME HAS COME FOR US TO LEAVE, WE BID YOU, ALL, <u>FAREWELL</u>

CLASS OF 1957
CARROLL HIGH SCHOOL
MONROE, LOUISIANA

EMD

THE NON-VIOLENT APPROACH DOES NOT IMMEDIATELY CHANGE THE HEART OF THE OPPRESSOR. IT, FIRST DOES SOMETHING TO THE HEARTS AND SOULS OF THOSE COMMITTED TO IT. IT GIVES THEM NEW SELF-RESPECT. IT CALLS UP RESOURCES AND STRENGTH THAT THEY DID NOT KNOW THEY HAD. FINALLY, IT REACHES THE OPPONENT AND SO STIRS HIS CONSCIENCE, THAT RECONCILIATION BECOMES A REALITY.

REV. MARTIN LUTHER KING, JR.

ANOTHER DAY

ANOTHER DAY OF HAPPINESS
ANOTHER DAY OF LOVE
ANOTHER DAY TO THANK THE LORD
FOR BLESSINGS FROM ABOVE.
ANOTHER DAY OF HAPPINESS
ANOTHER DAY OF CARE
ANOTHER DAY OF FINDING JOY
AND BOWING DOWN IN PRAYER
ANOTHER DAY OF HAPPINESS
ANOTHER DAY TO CALL ON GOD
AND FIND THE STRENGTH TO COPE
ANOTHER DAY OF HAPPINESS
ANOTHER DAY OF PEACE
ANOTHER DAY TO SERVE THE LORD
AND FIND OUR SWEET RELEASE.

HOPE C. OBERHELMAN

WHERE'S THE REST OF ME by RONALD REAGAN

THE STORY BEGINS WITH THE CLOSEUP OF A BOTTOM IN A SMALL TOWN, CALLED TAMPICO, IN ILLINOIS, ON FEBRUARY 6, 1911. MY FACE WAS BLUE FROM SCREAMING, MY BOTTOM WAS RED FROM WHACKING AND MY FATHER CLAIMED AFTERWARD, THAT HE WAS WHITE. EVER SINCE MY BIRTH, I HAVE BEEN PARTICULARILY FOND OF THE COLORS THAT WERE EXHIBITED, RED, WHITE AND BLUE. I HAVE NOT BEEN UNCOMFORTABLE ON THE VARIOUS OCASSIONS, WHEN I HAVE HAD AN OVERWHELMING IMPULSE TO BRANDISH THEM. I HAVE HEARD MORE THAN ONE PSYCHIATRIST SAY THAT WE IMBIBE OUR IDEALS FROM OUR MOTHER'S MILK. THEN, I MUST SAY, MY BREAST FEEDING WAS THE HOME OF THE BRAVE BABY AND THE FREE BOSOM. I WAS THE HUNGRIEST PERSON IN THE HOUSE, BUT, I, ONLY GOT CHUBBY WHEN I EXERCISED IN THE CRIB. ANY TIME I WASN'T GNAWING ON THE BARS, I WAS WORRING WITH MY THUMB IN MY MOUTH, HABITS WHICH HAVE, SYMBOLICALLY, PERSISTED THROUGHOUT MY LIFE.

IN 1954, REAGAN WAS HIRED AS HOST FOR THE TELEVISION SERIES, GENERAL ELECTRIC THEATER. HE TOURED FOR THE COMPANY TO ITS 135 PLANTS ACROSS THE COUNTRY, SPEAKING ON BEHALF OF THE COMPANY TO THE EMPLOYEES. "THE TRIPS WERE MURDEROUSLY DIFFICULT." BUT, I ENJOYED EVERY MINUTE OF IT. I HAD AN AWESOME SHIVERING FEELING THAT AMERICA WAS MAKING A PERSONAL APPEARANCE FOR ME, AND IT MADE ME THE BIGGEST FAN IN THE WORLD.'

AN INTERVIEW WITH A GOVERNOR

IN YOUR OWN WORDS, HOW IS IT POSSIBLE THAT A STATE LIKE CALIFORNIA CAN APPEAR SO REPUBLICAN, YET BE SO DEMOCRATIC, AS EVIDENCED IN THE FACT THAT ALTHOUGH MOST OF THE STATE'S DEMOCRATIC VOTING REGISTRANTS MAKE A GOOD SHOWING AT THE POLLS, ONLY TO HAVE REPUBLICANS WIN THE ELECTIONS? CROSS-FILING PRESENTS A VAGUE PICTURE OF A POLITICAL CANDIDATE. EVEN THE BIBLE NOTES THAT GOD WANTS TOTAL ALLEGIANCE AND A STRADDLE-THE-FENCE SORT OF IDENTIFICATION IS NOT ACCEPTABLE, MORALLY OR ETHICALLY, HOW IS IT THAT A STATE PICTURED AS THE EPITOME OF EVERY THING CLEAN AND LAWFUL COULD BE SO POLITICALLY CORRUPT AS TO EVEN ALLOW A SYSTEM OF CROSS-FILING BY CANDIDATES' DECLARATION OF PARTY AFFILIATION?

DO YOU FEEL THAT, ALTHOUGH THE SYSTEM SEEMED, BOTH, MORALLY AND ETHICALLY CORRUPT, ITS END RESULTS COULD LEAD TO AN EVEN MORE DEMOCRATIC STATE OF AFFAIRS EVEN WITH REPUBLICANS IN CONTROL AS A PARTY? WHY DO YOU FEEL GOVERNOR PAT BROWN WAS SUCH A DAMNED IF YOU DO AND DAMNED IF YOU DON'T KIND OF FIGURE FOR THE CONSTITUENTS IN HIS TERMS AS GOVERNOR OF CALIFORNIA? DO YOU THINK IT WAS FAIR OF THE PEOPLE TO REFLECT THEIR OWN NEGATIVE OR AMBIVALENT ENERGIES TOWARD THE GOVERNOR? AFTERALL, THE PREVIOUS YEARS OF SHADY FILING OF CANDIDACIES LEFT THE STATE IN PRETTY MUCH A "DOG YOU IF YOU DO AND DOG YOU IF YOU DON'T" WAY OF LOOKING AT THEIR CHOICE OF GOVERNOR.

GOVERNOR BROWN DID A LOT TO CHANGE THE COURSE THAT CALIFORNIA WAS TAKING. I DON'T BELIEVE KNOWLAND OR NIXON WOULD DISAGREE. SO, HOW IS IT THAT HE WAS SEEN ABOVE THE LAW BY SOME, NOT LAWFUL ENOUGH BY OTHERS INSPITE OF HIS CREDENTIALS AS STATE ATTORNEY GENERAL? HOW DO YOU FEEL CALIFORNIA WAS AFFECTED PERMANENTLY, BY PROSTITUTION? HOW DO YOU FEEL CALIFORNIA WAS AFFECTED, PERMANENTLY, BY ORGANIZED GAMBLING IN THE STATE?

I, PERSONALLY, REMEMBER CALIFORNIA'S WATER PROBLEM AND HOW IT WAS DEALT WITH, I ALSO, REMEMBER THAT IT WAS SIGNIFICANT AT A TIME WHEN CALIFORNIA WAS SERIOUSLY DEBATING THE ISSUE OF DIVIDING THE STATE INTO TWO STATES, THAT OF NORTHERN AND SOUTHERN CALIFORNIA. THE INSTITUTION OF AQUADUCTS AND CANALS TO SOLVE THE WATER PROBLEM WOULD MAKE DIVIDING THE STATE ALONG OPPOSITE DIRECTIONS UNFEASIBLE. SO, THE STATE REMAINS ONE STATE, UNDEVIDED, BUT, BECAUSE OF THE NEW INTERSTATE 5 HIGHWAY ALONG THE SAME ROUTE AS THE AQUADUCTS AND CANALS. DO YOU FEEL CALIFORNIA CAN BLAME SOME OF HER PROBLEMS, SUCH AS, ORGANIZED GAMBLING, POLITICAL CORRUPTION AND PROSTITUTION DIRECTLY ON THE YEARS PRECEEDING THE FAMED GOLD RUSH OR SHORTLY AFTER THE LEWIS AND CLARK EXPLORATION OF THE AREA, WEST? AFTERALL, CORRUPT HANDLING OF THE AREA OF NEW ORLEANS CONTINUED UNTIL SOMEONE, ALMOST, BEGGED TO HAVE THE AREA TAKEN OFF THEIR HANDS, THUS, RESULTING IN THE WHOLE TERRITORY BECOMING A PART OF THE SALE.

EVEN THEN, WATER SEEMED TO BE A CRITICAL MATTER, NEEDING ATTENTION, AS IT WAS NEW ORLEANS WAS AN IMPORTANT PORT AND THE MISSISSIPPI RIVER, CONNECTING WITH THE MISSOURI RIVER AND BECOMING A STARTING POINT FOR THE EXPEDITION, WOULD LEAD THE EXPLORERS WEST TO, STILL, MORE WATER, THE PACIFIC OCEAN.

THE FREEWAY SYSTEM WAS STEPPED-UP BY BROWN'S POLICY, THE UNIVERSITY AND COLLEGE SYSTEMS WERE STEPPED-UP UNDER HIS ADMINISTRATION. HE WAS, PERSONNALY, OPPOSED TO THE DEATH PENALTY AND WILL NOT SAY THAT HE MURDERED CARL CHESSMAN. PROSTITUTION AND GAMBLING WERE MORE CONTROLLED, THE RUMFORD FAIR HOUSING BILL WAS PASSED, THE LABOR ISSUE TOOK ON A NEW LOOK AND A RENEWED INTEREST IN MIGRANT WORKERS WAS MADE. WOULD YOU AGREE THAT ALL THIS SOUNDS VERY PROGRESSIVE AND, THUS, FAVORABLE FOR A GOVERNOR? HOW IS IT, THEN, THAT SOME, SAW HIS TENURE AS A FALURE, EVEN SAYING THAT HE MOVED TO SWIFTLY AND COMPLETELY IN SOME CASES?

DURING EDMOND G. BROWN'S EIGHT YEARS AS GOVERNOR OF CALIFORNIA, THE STATE UNDERWENT A SERIES OF REVOLUTIONS, SOME OF THESE BEING POPULATION EXPLOSION, STUDENT REVOLT IN BERKELEY, MIGRANT FARM WORKERS, RACE RIOTS AND WHITE BACKLASH. THE TERM, "PEOPLE WANT A PAUSE" WAS USED TO DESCRIBE THE MOOD OF THE PEOPLE AS GOVERNOR BROWN WAS EJECTED FROM OFFICE AFTER HIS DEFEAT FOR A THIRD TERM.

IN SEPTEMBER 1966, A RIOT ERUPTED IN THE HUNTERS POINT AREA OF SAN FRANCISCO OVER THE SHOOTING OF A SIXTEEN YEAR OLD BOY SUSPECTED OF AUTOMOBILE THEFT. EVEN THOUGH THE NEGRO POPULATION OF SAN FRANCISCO, LOCATED MAINLY IN THE GHETTO AREAS OF HUNTERS POINT AND THE FILMORE DISTRICT, WAS AROUND 80,000 JUST BEFORE THE ELECTION OF RONALD REAGAN, IT WAS ENOUGH TO INITIATE A RIOT, SIMILAR IN SEVERAL WAYS TO THE WATTS RIOT IN SOUTHERN CALIFORNIA. EVEN SO, THERE WERE VERY OBVIOUS DISSIMILARITIES IN THE TWO CALIFORNIA RIOT SITUATIONS. WHAT GUBERNATORIAL CANDIDATE COULD RESIST THE TEMPTATION TO EXPLOIT THE RIOT FOR A VOT-GETTING MEANS? IT IS SAID THAT MR. REAGAN HEDGEHOPPED ACROSS CALIFORNIA AND AT EVERY STOP DEPLORED NEGRO UNREST, BUT, DENIED THE OBVIOUS WHITE BACKLASH. HOW IMPORTANT IS WHITE BACKLASH IN CAMPAIGN STRATEGY?

NEWSPAPERS, SUCH AS THE SAN FRANCISCO CHRONICLE AND EXAMINER, THE SANTA BARBARA NEWS, SAN LUIS OBISPO TRIBUNE, SACRAMENTO, MODESTO AND FRESNO BEES AND LOS ANGELES HERALD-EXAMINER GAVE THEIR VOTE TO GOVERNOR BROWN, WHILE PAPERS, SUCH AS SAN JOSE MERCURY NEWS, SAN MATEO TIMES, OAKLAND TRIBUNE, SANTA ANA REGISTER, HAYWARD PRESS, GAVE THEIR VOTE TO CANDIDATE REAGAN. HOW IMPORTANT IS THE VOTE FROM THE NEWSPAPER COMMUNITY? IS IT MORE IMPORTANT THAN THE CLOUT OF THE LABOR UNIONS?

EX-CONGRESSWOMAN, SHIRLEY CHISLOM IS REMEMBERED FOR HER SLOGAN, "UNBOUGHT AND UNBIASED", AS A WAY TO DESCRIBE HER, POLITICALLY. WOULD YOU, NOT AGREE THAT THIS IS VASTLY DIFFERENT PICTURE THAN THAT OF MR. REAGAN IN HIS ORIGINAL CANDIDACY, WHEN HE IS SAID TO HAVE RESEMBLED A CAREFULLY DESIGNED, ELABORATELY CUSTOMIZED SUPERMARKET PACKAGE, COMPLETE WITH THE GLOSSIEST WRAPPING AND THE SLICKEST SORT OF EYE APPEAL? WHY WAS BLACK POWER FREIGHTENING WHEN BLACKS, SUCH AS STOKELY CARMICHAEL, USED IT?

LYNDON JOHNSON WAS NOT A FREQUENT CAMPAIGN BACKER FOR THE STATE OF CALIFORNIA, EVEN THOUGH THE STATE WAS ATTRACTIVE TO, BOTH, CONSERVATIVES AND LIBERALS, ALIKE, ACROSS THE COUNTRY. WHY DO YOU THINK THIS IS SO? COULD IT BE THAT, EVEN THEN, THE STATE OF TEXAS WAS BEING READIED FOR WHAT IT IS TODAY, A NEW MICROCROSM OF THE U.S.? RONALD REAGAN SEEMED TO THINK THAT THE WORD, INTEGRITY WAS STILL A GOOD WORD IN HIS CAMPAIGN OF 1966 AND I WOULD TEND TO AGREE, AT THAT TIME, ALSO, (I WAS A CASHIER AT THE TWENTY-SEVENTH AND TELE-GRAPH SEARS ROEBUCK LOCATION AND SAW ALL SORTS OF FACES, AT A TIME WHEN SOME PEOPLE STILL FELT THAT ALL BLACKS WERE THIEVES AND COULDN'T BE TRUSTED WITH THE STORE'S RECEIPTS).

PEOPLE WERE BOUND WITH SOCIAL UNREST, ANXIETY AND CONFUSION AND PROTEST, INSTEAD OF PRAISE, WAS ON THE LIPS OF MANY. MY FAVORITE PLACE TO BE AT THE TIME WAS ON A PIC-NIC BLANKET AROUND THE BEAUTIFUL LAKE MERRIT AND THEN CAME THE DRUG LORDS AND FAIRYLAND WAS NEVER TO BE THE SAME, AGAIN. IT WENT THE WAY OF PIONEER VILLAGE, A CHILD'S FANTASY IN SAN JOSE. NOTHING GOOD LASTS FOREVER. DO YOU FEEL REAGAN WON THE ELECTION AT ALL, BECAUSE OF HIS INTEGRITY? AFTERALL, IT WAS NOT NESCESSARY AS PAT BROWN HAD EXHIBITED IN HIS CAMPAIGN BIDS. I SAW THE MOVIE, 'THE LAST BOYSCOUT' DOZENS OF TIMES, STARRING BRUCE WILLIS AND DAMAN WAYANS. THE CAMPAIGN FIGURE IN THIS MOVIE REMINDED ME A LOT OF THE REAL LIFE CAMPAIGNER, PAT BROWN; WOULD YOU AGREE? THERE WAS ENOUGH CORRUPTION TO BURY THE WHOLE LOT. 'NO WAY OUT' WAS ANOTHER FILM, DEPICTING SO MUCH POLITICAL CORRUPTION. WOULD YOU AGREE? THIS ENDS MY INTERVIEW WITH A GOVERNOR. IF I WERE TO INTERVIEW A MAYOR, FOR MORE LOCAL INTEREST, IT WOULD NOT BE MAYORS, YORTY, BRADLEY, FEINSTEIN OR ALIOTA. IT WOULD BE MAYOR WILLIE BROWN AND THEN I WOULD BE WELL CONVINCED THAT THE SOUTH WAS, INDEED, BEING READIED TO RISE, AGAIN. ANYWAY, IF YOU REMOVED NEW YORK, LOUISIANA AND CALIFORNIA FROM MY LIFE, I WOULD NOT HAVE ANY. THERE IS A KIND OF SADNESS CAUGHT UP IN REVOLUTIONS. ONE KNOWS THAT CHANGE IS INEVITIABLE, BUT, SOMETHING ALWAYS DIES, ALONG WITH THE PEOPLE AND THIS IS SAD, BUT, TRUE.

EMD

STATE: CALIFORNIA

ADMISSION: 31st

MOTTO: EUREKA

SONG: I LOVE YOU, CALIFORNIA

MINERAL: GOLD

FLOWER: CALIFORNIA POPPY

FLAG: BEAR FLAG

TREE: THE REDWOOD

CALIFORNIA WAS THE ONLY WESTERN STATE TO SKIP, ENTIRELY, THE STEP OF BEING A TERRITORY.

A YEAR AFTER ITS OFFICIAL ADOPTION, MEMBERS OF THE STATE LEGISLATURE WERE POLLED TO SEE HOW MANY COULD RECALL, BOTH, TUNE AND LYRIC TO THE SONG, CALIFORNIA, I LOVE YOU. ONLY ONE MEMBER OF THE LEGISLATURE COULD RECALL THE TUNE OR LYRICS.

THE EMBLEM ON THE OFFICIAL FLAG OF CALIFORNIA WAS THE GRIZZLY, WHICH BORE THE MARVELOUS LATIN NAME, URSUS HORRIBILIS CALIFORNICUS. THE LAST KNOWN MEMBER OF THE SPECIES WAS KILLED IN 1927.

THE SEQUOIA SEMPERVIRENS IS BETTER KNOWN AS THE COAST REDWOOD, WHICH IS

(OVER)

A SPECIES OF CONE-BEARING EVERGREEN NATIVE TO A SMALL PART THE RAIN SWEPT PACIFIC COAST OF THE NORTH AMERICAN CONTINENT. IT WAS ALSO THE TALLEST LIVING THING IN THE WORLD. AND IT WAS LOCATED ON ONE OF THE MOST BEAUTIFUL RIVER FLATS IN NORTHERN CALIFORNIA AT THE CONFLUENCE OF REDWOOD AND BOND CREEKS.

THE MEXICAN-AMERICAN WORKER

THERE WAS THE PATTERN ESTABLISHED. CAREY WcWILLIAMS, ONE TIME CALIFORNIA COMMISSIONER OF HOUSING AND IMMIGRATION SAW IT AS FOLLOWS, "TO BRING IN SUCCESSFUL MINORITY GROUPS, TO EXPLOIT THEM UNTIL THE ADVANTAGES OF EXPLOITATION HAVE BEEN EXHAUSTED AND THEN TO EXPEL THEM IN FAVOR OF MORE READILY EXPLOITABLE MATERIAL".

EARTHQUAKES

ELASTIC REBOUND, THE DEAD RISING, SINS OR FAULTS?

SOME EARTHQUAKES ARE NOT FELT (NOT CONSCIOUSLY FELT) BY MAN, BUT ARE, STILL, RECORDABLE WITH THE USE OF SEISMIC INSTRUMENTS. THE EARTHQUAKE SOUND IS LIKE A LOW-PITCHED MOAN OR LIKE MANY FREIGHT TRAINS. THE "CIRCLE OF FIRE" IS A GROUP OF FAULTS AROUND THE PACIFIC BASIN, A SEISMIC BELT.

(OVER)

EARTHQUAKES (CON'D)

THE "SMITH LETTER"

IN A RANGER STATION NEAR MOUNT SHASTER A FORESTRY SUPERVISOR, NAMED GYPSUM P. SMITH, ADDED A FEW FINAL LINES TO A LETTER TO HIS SISTER IN BALTIMORE, WHICH READ, "CURIOUS THINGS HAVE BEEN HAPPENING. LAST NIGHT, JUST BEFORE I WENT TO BED, MY DOG, SPOT, BEGAN WHIMPERING AND SHIVERING. I LOOKED OUTSIDE, THINKING A BEAR MIGHT HAVE WANDERED INTO CAMP, BUT, SAW NOTHING. SHORTLY AFTER DAWN, THERE WAS A TERRIBLE HOWLING, AS IF EVERY COYOTE IN THE AREA HAD DECIDED TO COMPLAIN AT THE SAME TIME. THEN, THIS MORNING, A LARGE NUMBER OF DEER, FAWNS, DOES AND BIG BUCKS WITH TREMENDOUS ANTLERS CAME RUNNING THROUGH THE CAMP, AS IF CHASED BY SOMETHING. SHORTLY AFTER THIS, I HEARD FROM FRANK, THAT DURING THE NIGHT THE TROUT OVER IN THE HATCHERY CLUSTERED IN THE EASTERN CORNER OF THE PONDS SO TIGHTLY, THAT WHEN DISCOVERED THIS MORNING, MANY OF THEM HAD SUFFOCATED. ANOTHER THING, PERHAPS UNRELATED, YESTERDAY, A RANGER NEAR SUSANVILLE REPORTED THE SKY WAS DARK WITH SEAGULLS. HE'D PROBABLY BEEN MUCH KIDDED, SINCE, TO MY KNOWLEDGE, GULLS ARE RARELY SEEN THIS FAR INLAND. AS I WROTE THE ABOVE, SPOT LET OUT THE MOST MOURNFUL HOUL. EVERYTHING HAS A LOGICAL EXPLANATION, OF COURSE. SPOT IS PROBABLY COMING

(OVER)

DOWN WITH A COLD. AND THE RANGER, WHO REPORTED SEEING THE GULLS, PROBABLY HAD TOO MUCH EARLY TIMES. STILL, WHY SHOULD THE FAMILIAR HOWL OF THE COYOTE, THE FREIGHTENED FLUTTER OF THE BIRDS AND THE UNEASE OF SOME OF MY FOREST FRIENDS, BOTHER ME? AND WHY, SO OFTEN, TODAY, HAVE I CAUGHT MYSELF PAUSING AND LISTENING? AND FOR WHAT?" THE LETTER WAS WRITTEN SEVEN DAYS BEFORE THE DISASTER.

I HAVE BLOTTED OUT, AS A THICK CLOUD, THY TRANSGRESSIONS, AND AS A CLOUD, THY SINS RETURN UNTO ME FOR I HAVE REDEEMED THE.

SING O YE HEAVENS FOR THE LORD HATH DONE IT, SHOUT, YE LOWER PARTS OF THE EARTH. BREAK FORTH INTO SINGING YE MOUNTAINS, O FOREST, AND EVERY TREE, THEREIN, FOR THE LORD HATH REDEEMED JACOB AND GLORIFIED HIMSELF IS ISRAEL.

THUS, SAITH THE LORD, THY REDEEMER AND HE THAT FORMED THEE FROM THE WOMB I AM THE LORD THAT MAKETH ALL THINGS, THAT STRETCHETH FORTH THE HEAVENS ALONE, THAT SPREADETH ABROAD, THE EARTH BY MYSELF.

THAT FRUSTRATETH THE TOKENS OF THE LIARS, AND MAKETH DIVINERS MAD, THAT TURNETH WISE MEN BACKWARD AND MAKETH THEIR KNOWLEDGE FOOLISH.

ISAIAH 44; 22-25

GRAPES OF WRATH OR ROTTING GRAPES?

CESAR ESTRADA CHAVEZ WAS BORN IN YUMA, ARIZONA IN 1927. HE CHERISHED A DEEPLY RELIGIOUS BELIEF IN THE DIGNITY OF THE HUMAN BEING. HE WAS A NATURAL MESSIANIC QUALITY. HE EMPHASIZED UNITY AND TAUGHT PRINCIPLES OF NON-VIOLENT PROTEST.

WHY WON'T THEY NEGOTIATE? ASKED THE STRIKERS. WHY WON'T THEY COME BACK TO WORK? ASKED THE GROWERS. WHAT THEY DON'T UNDERSTAND, CHAVEZ TOLD A SAN FRANCISCO REPORTER, IS WE'RE COMMITTED, YOU SEE. WHEN YOU LOSE YOUR CAR, THEN LOSE YOUR HOME, YOU DON'T BECOME LESS COMMITTED, BUT, MORE. NONE OF US, NOW, HAVE ANYTHING TO LOSE.

"DAD, WILL YOU TEACH ME HOW TO FIGHT?"
ROCKY

"WE DON'T BELONG DOWN HERE, ANYWAY"
THREE AMIGOS

"I DO SO WITH GREAT PLEASURE"
TERMINAL VELOCITY

"THIS IS YOUR CHANCE OF A LIFETIME"
THE HIGH AND MIGHTY

"IT MEANS YOU ARE READY TO REJOIN SOCIETY"
SHAWSHANK REDEMPTION

"I KNEW THAT THIS WAS A GOOD IDEA"
WATERBOY

I HAD A LITTLE BEFORE THE HURRICANES AND NOW AFTERWARDS, I HAVE EVEN LESS WHY DOES GOD LET PEOPLE SUFFER?

A GUEST ON CNN'S
DR. PHIL SHOW SHORTLY
AFTER HURRICANE KATRINA

MANY PEOPLE TURN TO GOD IN TRAGIC SITUATIONS, WHETHER IT'S IN A MASS OCCURANCE LIKE THE WEATHER STORMS OR ALONE SITUATIONS, SUCH AS ONE MINUTE TO GAS CHAMBER OR ELECTRIC CHAIR OR IN THE BACK OF AN AMBULANCE, HELPLESS AS THE DAY YOU WERE BORN. GOD CREATED THE HEAVENS AND EARTH BEFORE HE DID US (WE ARE FINITE IN OUR BEING, SO WE MUST HAVE A BEGINNING. WE NEVER STOP TO THANK A GRACIOUS GOD FOR ALLOWING US TO WALK UPRIGHT OR TRED UPON HIS EARTH. UNDERFOOT IS WHERE IT IS, BUT, IT IS AS IMPORTANT AS THE HEAVEN, ABOVE. EVEN THIS, GOD SAID WILL PASS AWAY, BUT, HE WILL REMAIN. EARTHQUAKES HAPPEN, STORMS HAPPEN, FLOODS HAPPEN AND FIRES HAPPEN. WOULD YOU NOT SAY THAT ALL CREATION SUFFERS AND GOD IS NOT JUST PICKING ON THE HUMAN PORTION? ALL OF CREATION GROANS, BUT, STILL THERE IS NO LOVE STORY LIKE THE ONE OF GOD AND HIS. IF, ONLY, WE WERE AS RESPONSIBLE FOR OURS AS HE IS FOR HIS,HIS EYE IS ON THE SPARROW, HE SEES THE MINNOW SWIM AND HE KNOWS OUR SORROWS AND HE TOUCHES OUR HEARTS TO HAVE YOU ASK THE QUESTION IN THE FIRST PLACE.

EMD

Lewis

Clark

"EVERY LAWYER ON THE FACE OF THE EARTH SHOULD BE KILLED" THE FIRM

"ANOTHER TRAGIC TALE OF WASTED YOUTH" THE LAST BOYSCOUT

"MY HUSBAND HAS BEEN DEAD FOR YEARS" DARE DEVIL

"YOU HAVE GOT TO GET ME SOMEONE WHO KNOWS WHAT SHE IS DOING" BIG

"SOUNDS LIKE YOU HAVE A SECRET ADMIRER, JOHN" DIE HARD WITH A VENGENANCE

"IT MEANS I CAN BUY ALL THE GAS I WANT" BOOTY CALL

"YOUR FATHER MIGHT BELONG IN PRISON" INSTINCT

Part 3

AND THE LORD DIRECT YOUR HEARTS INTO THE LOVE OF GOD AND INTO THE PATIENT WAITING FOR CHRIST.

2 THESSALONIANS 3:5

DRINK NO LONGER WATER, BUT, USE A LITTLE WINE FOR THE STOMACH'S SAKE AND THINE OFTEN INFIRMITIES.

1 TIMOTHY 5:23

PREACH THE WORD BE INSTANT IN SEASON OUT OF SEASON REPROVE, REBUKE, EXHORT, WITH ALL LONG SUFFERING AND DOCTRINE.

2 TIMOTHY 4:2

WHOSOEVER SHALL DENY ME BEFORE MEN, HIM WILL I ALSO DENY, BEFORE MY FATHER WHICH IS IN HEAVEN.

MATTHEW 10:32

FOR WHEN THEY SHALL RISE FROM THE DEAD, THEY NEITHER MARRY NOR ARE GIVEN IN MARRIAGE, BUT, ARE AS THE ANGELS WHICH ARE IN HEAVEN.

MARK 12:25

FOR I SAY UNTO YOU THAT THIS THAT IS WRITTEN, MUST, YET, BE ACCOMPLISHED IN ME AND HE WAS RECKONED AMONG THE TRANSGRESSORS, FOR THE THINGS CONCERNING ME, HAVE AN END.

LUKE 22:37

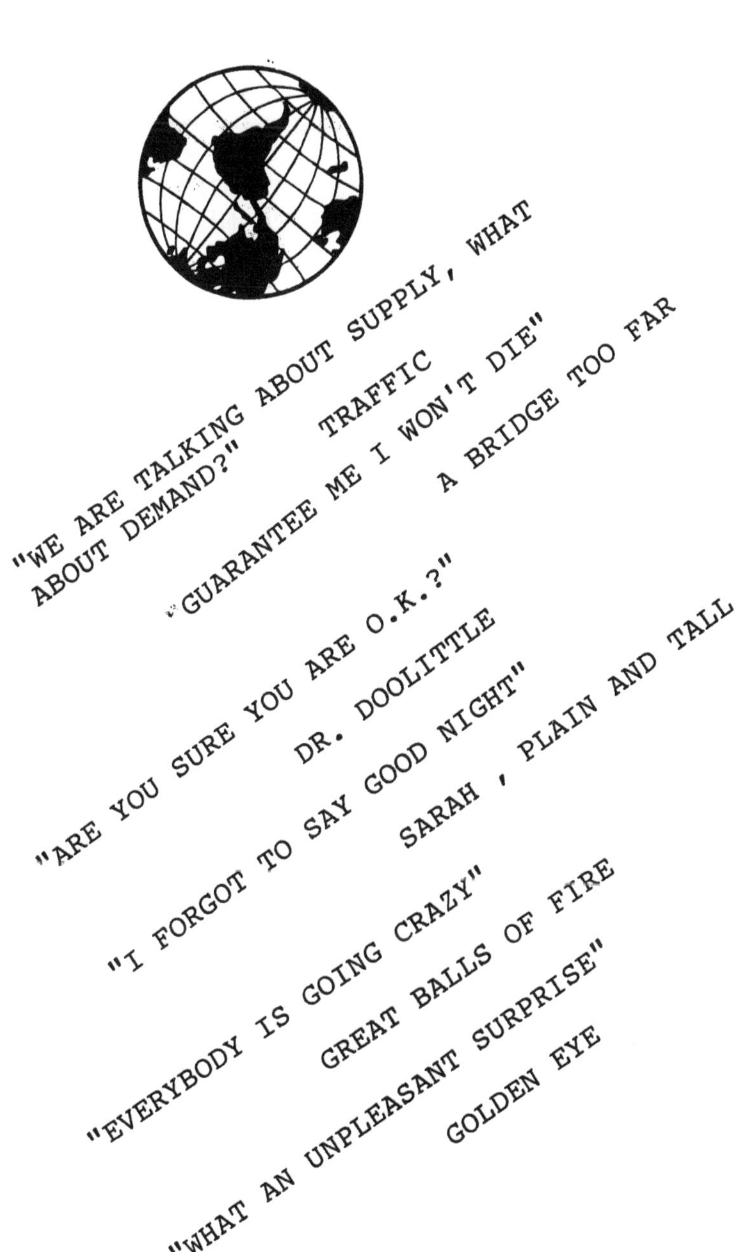
"WE ARE TALKING ABOUT SUPPLY, WHAT
ABOUT DEMAND?"
TRAFFIC
"GUARANTEE ME I WON'T DIE"
A BRIDGE TOO FAR
"ARE YOU SURE YOU ARE O.K.?"
DR. DOOLITTLE
"I FORGOT TO SAY GOOD NIGHT"
SARAH , PLAIN AND TALL
"EVERYBODY IS GOING CRAZY"
GREAT BALLS OF FIRE
"WHAT AN UNPLEASANT SURPRISE"
GOLDEN EYE

THE LORD IS MY SHEPHERD, I SHALL NOT WANT, HE MAKETH ME TO LIE DOWN IN GREEN PASTURES, HE LEADETH ME BESIDE THE STILL WATERS, HE RESTORETH MY SOUL, HE LEADETH ME IN PATHS OF RIGHTEOUSNESS FOR HIS NAME'S SAKE, YEA THOUGH I WALK THRU THE FALLEY OF THE SHADOW OF DEATH, I WILL FEAR NO EVIL, FOR THOU ART WITH ME, THY ROD AND THY STAFF, THEY COMFORT ME, THOU PREPAREST A TABLE BEFORE ME IN THE PRESENCE OF MINE ENIMIES, THOU ANOINTEST MY HEAD WITH OIL, MY CUP RENNETH OVER, SURELY GOODNESS AND MERCY SHALL FOLLOW ME ALL THE DAYS OF MY LIFE AND I WILL DWELL IN THE HOUSE OF THE LORD, FOREVER.

PSALM 23

REUBEN, SIMEON, LEVI, JUDAH, ZEBULUN, ISSACHAR, DAN, GAD, ASHER, NAPHTALI, JOSEPH AND BENJAMIN.

GENESIS 49:3-27

REUBEN, THOU ART MY FIRSTBORN, MY MIGHT AND THE BEGINNING OF MY STRENGTH, THE EXCELLENCY OF POWER.

GENESIS 49:3

"I'M ABOUT FOUR MILES AHEAD OF YOU, TURKEY". SMOKEY AND THE BANDIT

"I'VE TOLD YOU AGAIN AND AGAIN, THEY COULDN'T HAVE DONE IT" THE SPY WHO CAME IN FROM THE COLD

"SHE LOOKS A LITTLE FAMILIAR" WHILE YOU WERE OUT

"BREAK IT WITH HIM BEFORE HE BREAKS IT WITH YOU" TWO CAN PLAY THAT GAME

HE HATH MADE EVERYTHING BEAUTIFUL: BEAUTIFUL IN HIS TIME. ALSO, HE HATH SET THE WORLD IN THEIR HEART.

ECCLESIASTES 3:11

EVEN THE LORD, GOD OF HOSTS, THE LORD IS HIS MEMORIAL.

HOSEA 12:5

BEHOLD, I HAVE MADE THEE SMALL AMONG THE HEATHEN, THOU ART GREATLY DESPISED.

OBADIAH 1:2

AND IT SHALL COME TO PASS AFTERWARDS, THAT I WILL POUR OUT MY SPIRIT UPON ALL FLESH AND YOUR SONS AND YOUR DAUGHTERS SHALL PROPHESY, YOUR OLD MEN SHALL DREAM DREAMS, YOUR YOUNG MEN SHALL SEE VISIONS.

JOEL 2:28

AND IT SHALL COME TO PASS IN THAT DAY SAITH THE LORD, GOD THAT I WILL CAUSE THE SUN TO GO DOWN AT NOON AND I WILL DARKEN THE EARTH IN THE CLEAR DAYS.

AMOS 8:9

PRIDE GOETH BEFORE A FALL
LIKE BIRDS FLOCKING TOGETHER,
A FISH OUT OF WATER
IS LIKE BEING CAUGHT
IN BAD WEATHER

EMD

PRAISE, YE THE LORD. PRAISE GOD IN HIS SANCTUARY, PRAISE HIM IN THE FIRMAMENT OF HIS POWER. PRAISE HIM FOR HIS MIGHTY ACTS, PRAISE HIM ACCORDING TO HIS EXCELLENT GREATNESS PRAISE HIM WITH THE SOUND OF THE TRUMPET. PRAISE HIM WITH THE TIMBREL AND DANCE, PRAISE HIM WITH STRINGED INSTRUMENTS AND ORGANS, PRAISE HIM UPON THE HIGH SOUNDING CYMBALS. LET EVERY THING THAT HATH BREATH, PRAISE THE LORD, PRAISE YE THE LORD.

PSALM 150

LOVE IS A POWER
THAT QUIETS A RAGING STORM
LOVE IS A POWER
THAT GENTLES A NEWBORN.

EMD

RUN, NOW, I PRAY, THEE, TO MEET HER, AND SAY UNTO HER, IS IT WELL WITH THEE? IS IT WELL WITH THY HUSBAND? IS IT WELL WITH WITH THY CHILD? AND SHE ANSWERED, IT IS WELL.

2 KINGS 4:26

BE MINDFUL ALWAYS OF HIS COVENANT, THE WORD WHICH HE COMMANDED TO A THOUSAND GENERATIONS.

1 chronicles 16:15

SO THERE WAS GREAT JOY IN JERUSALEM FOR SINCE THE TIME OF SOLOMON, THE SON OF DAVID, KING OF ISRAEL, THERE WAS NOT THE LIKEIN JERUSALEM. THEN THE PRIESTS, THE LEVITES AROSE AND BLESSED THE PEOPLE AND THEIR VOICE WAS HEARD AND THEIR PRAYER CAME UP TO HIS HOLY DWELLING PLACE UNTO HEAVEN.

2 CHRONICLES
30: 26,27

A STILLBORN CHILD EMD

I CAME, I LEFT
IN ONE QUICK INSTANT
SO QUICK, I CAN'T
SEPARATE THE BIRTH
THING FROM THE DEATH THING
DID I MISS SOMETHING?
I THINK NOT,
FOR COMPLETE IS COMPLETE
AS FULL IS FULL
I AM COMPLETE.

THEN JONAH PRAYED UNTO THE LORD,
HIS GOD OUT OF THE FISH'S BELLY.

JONAH 2:1

THOU SHALT KNOW HIM WHEN HE COMES
THOU SHALT KNOW HIM WHEN HE COMES
NOT BY ANY DIN OF DRUMS
NOR THE VANTAGE OF HIS AIRS
NOR BY ANYTHING HE WEARS
NEITHER BY HIS CROWN
BUT, HIS PRESENCE KNOWN SHALL BE
BY THE HOLY HARMONY
WHICH HIS COMING MAKES IN THEE.

ANONYMOUS

A SOUL'S MISSION

FROM THE WATERY GRAVE OF MY
MOTHER'S WOMB,
TO THE SILENT NOTHINGNESS
OF OLD EARTH'S TOMB

FROM THE EVER CHANGING
OFTEN FLEETING SPHERE
I GRASP FOR THE STRAWS
AS EVIDENCE OF BEING HERE.

THE NAKEDNESS I BROUGHT
IS MINE, ONLY TO WILL
TO SIMPLY RETURN ONE DAY
TO A PLACE SO STILL.

EMD

I WILL PRAISE THEE WITH MY WHOLE HEART, BEFORE THE GODS, I WILL SING PRAISE UNTO THEE. I WILL WORSHIP TOWARD THY HOLY TEMPLE AND PRAISE THY NAME FOR THY LOVING KINDNESS AND FOR THY TRUTH. FOR THOU HAST MAGNIFIED THY WORD ABOVE ALL THY NAME. IN THE DAY WHEN I CRIED, THOU ANSWEREDST WITH STRENGTH IN MY SOUL. ALL THE KINGS OF THE EARTH SHALL PRAISE THEE O LORD, WHEN THEY HEAR THE WORDS OF THY MOUTH. YEA THEY SHALL SING GREAT IS THE GLORY OF THE LORD. THOUGH THE LORD BE HIGH, YET HATH HE RESPECT UNTO THE LOWLY BUT THE PROUD HE KNOWTH AFAR OFF. THOUGH I WALK IN THE MIDST OF TROUBLE, THOU SHALT STRETCH FORTH THINE HAND AND THY RIGHT HAND SHALL SAVE ME. THE LORD WILL PERFECT THAT WHICH CONCERNETH ME. THY MERCY O LORD ENDURETH FOREVER. FORSAKE NOT THE WORKS OF THINE OWN HANDS.

PSALM 138

I CALLED UPON THY NAME, O LORD, OUT OF THE LOW DUNGEON.

LAMENTATIONS 3:55

FOR SO AN ENTRANCE SHALL BE MINISTERED UNTO YOU ABUNDANTLY INTO THE EVERLASTING KINGDON OF OUR LORD AND SAVIOUR, JESUS CHRIST.

2 PETER 1:11

AND HEREBY WE DO KNOW THAT WE KNOW HIM , IF WE KEEP HIS COMMANDMENTS.

1 JOHN 2:3

AND THIS IS LOVE, THAT WE WALK AFTER HIS COMMANDMENTS. THIS IS THE COMMANDMENT, THAT AS YE HAVE HEARD FROM THE BEGINNING, YE SHOULD WALK IN IT.

2 JOHN 1:6

I HAVE NO GREATER JOY THAN TO HEAR THAT MY CHILDREN WALK IN TRUTH.

3 JOHN 1:4

BUT, BELOVED, REMEMBER YE THE WORDS WHICH WERE SPOKEN BEFORE, OF THE APOSTLES OF THE LORD JESUS CHRIST

JUDE 1:17

AND BELOVED I COME QUICKLY AND MY REWARD IS WITH ME TO GIVE EVERY MAN ACCORDING AS HIS WORK SHALL BE.

REVELATION 22:12

AN EASTER NOTE:
THE THING TO REMEMBER IS NOT THAT HE WAS RAISED OR THAT HE AROSE, BUT, THAT HE IS RISEN, FOREVER.

SOMETHING FOR THE IMAGINATION:
IMAGINE A FRAIL LITTLE OLD LADY WITH HER CROCHETED HAT, HER EMBROIDERED SHAWL AND HER LACE HANKY. SHE HAS FINE STATIONERY, A PEN AND INK WITH WHICH TO WRITE. NOW IMAGINE WHAT GOD IS AND WHAT HE MEANT WHEN HE SAID HE WOULD "WRITE IT (HIS COMMANDMENTS) UPON THE HEARTS OF MEN."

I LOVE TO RECALL FAITH PASSAGES OF SCRIPTURE. ONE OF MY FAVORITES IS WHERE THE TWO BLIND MEN SAT AND "SAW" JESUS PASS ON HIS WAY TO HIS DESTINATION. THEY SAID "MASTER, GIVE US YOUR SIGHT BECAUSE WHERE YOU ARE GOING, YOU WON'T NEED IT." THEY WERE BLIND IN THEIR BODY OF FLESH, BUT, THEY COULD "SEE" JESUS FOR WHO HE, REALLY WAS AND THEY KNEW THAT HIS BODY OF FLESH WAS JUST TEMPORARY AND WITH THAT, THE REALITY OF GOD WAS HIM, EVERLASTING, AS EVIDENCED BY JESUS' OWN SAYING TO THOSE IN THE SACRED PLACE AS HE SAID, "DESTROY THIS TEMPLE AND IN THREE DAYS I WILL RAISE IT UP, AGAIN."

EMD

IT IS NOT POSSIBLE TO BE SAVED AND NOT KNOW THAT YOU ARE SAVED, BUT, IT IS POSSIBLE TO NOT BE SAVED AND NOT KNOW THAT YOU ARE NOT SAVED.

EMD

THE ARC OF SAFETY IS THE ARC THAT JESUS BUILT WHEN GOD TOLD NOAH TO COME WITH HIS FAMILY. THE ARC OF SAFETY IS THE PLACE WHERE WE COME WHEN WE HEAR THE INVITATION TO COME ABOARD. THE ARC OF SAFETY IS THE LINEAGE OF ABRAHAM AND THE HOUSE OF DAVID THAT SERVES THE LORD.

EMD

THE UNIVERSE IS A LOT OF SPACE
IT CAN BE VERY DARK, VERY LONELY
THE WORLD IS A BIG PLACE
IT CAN BE VERY CRUEL SOMETIMES
BUT, THE ARC IS NOT ONLY SAFE
IT IS LIGHT, IT IS FRIENDLY
IT IS THE HOME FOR YOU AND ME
THAT WAS PREPARED BY JESUS, ALONE.

EMD

ENLIGHTEN THE PEOPLE, GENERALLY, AND TYRANNY AND OPRESSION OF BODY AND MIND WILL VANISH LIKE EVIL SPIRITS AT THE DAWN OF DAY.

THOMAS JEFFERSON

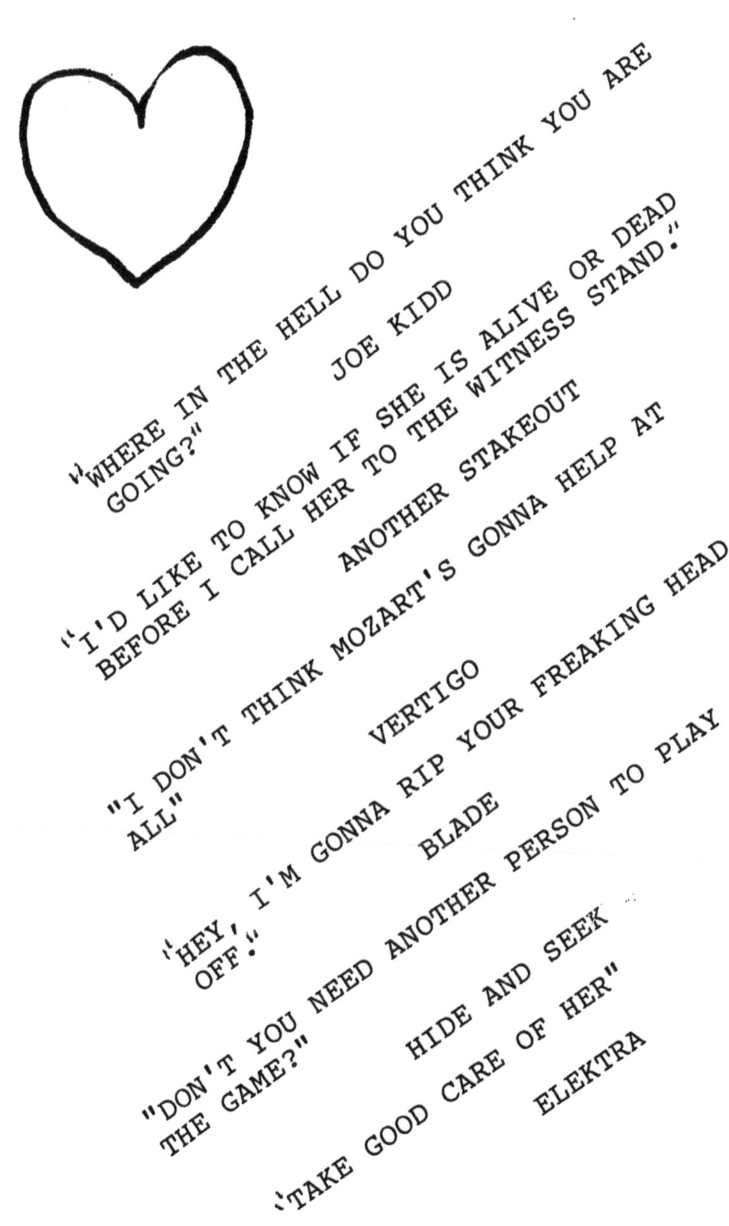
"WHERE IN THE HELL DO YOU THINK YOU ARE GOING?"
JOE KIDD
"I'D LIKE TO KNOW IF SHE IS ALIVE OR DEAD BEFORE I CALL HER TO THE WITNESS STAND."
ANOTHER STAKEOUT
"I DON'T THINK MOZART'S GONNA HELP AT ALL"
VERTIGO
"HEY, I'M GONNA RIP YOUR FREAKING HEAD OFF!"
BLADE
"DON'T YOU NEED ANOTHER PERSON TO PLAY THE GAME?"
HIDE AND SEEK
"TAKE GOOD CARE OF HER"
ELEKTRA

A FRIEND OWES KINDNESS TO
ONE IN DESPAIR...JOB 6:14

THE GIFT OF FRIENDSHIP

FRIENDSHIP IS GOD-GIVEN
A GIFT FOR YOU AND ME,
AND IF WE USE IT WISELY
WHAT A TREASURE IT CAN BE
IF WE CAN SPEAK TO SOMEONE
WHO NEEDS A WORD OF CHEER
OR OFFER LOVING COMFORT
TO SOMEONE FAR OR NEAR
THEN WE FOLLOW IN HIS FOOT-
STEPS AND FIND THE WELCOME GRACE
THAT COMES WHEN, WITH A GESTURE
WE CAN, EASILY, ERASE
SOMEONE'S CARE AND SORROW
THAT UNHAPPINESS IMPARTS
AND OUR LIVES WILL BE MUCH RICHER
WHEN WE FREELY GIVE OUR HEARTS

JEAN C. SOULE

MY LOVE FOR YOU

A ROSE WILL BLOOM, THEN WITHER
IT'S PETALS, FALL AWAY
UNLIKE THE LOVE I HAVE FOR YOU
THAT THRIVES AND GROWS EACH DAY
A DREAM LASTS ONLY SECONDS
AND THEN IS GONE AND OVER
UNLIKE THE LOVE I HAVE FOR YOU
THAT WILL LAST EVERMORE
THE WAVES WASH IN UPON BEACH
SAND CASTLES WASH AWAY
UNLIKE THE LOVE I HAVE FOR YOU
MOST STEADFAST, DAY BY DAY
THE SEASONS COME, THE SEASONS GO
AS THEY ARE BOUND TO DO
UNLIKE THE LOVE WITHIN MY HEART
THAT LIVES EACH DAY ANEW.

AND MOSES SAID UNTO GOD, BEHOLD, WHEN I COME UNTO THE CHILDREN OF ISRAEL AND SHALL SAY UNTO THEM, THE GOD OF YOUR FATHERS HATH SENT ME UNTO YOU AND THEY SHALL SAY TO ME, WHAT IS HIS NAME? WHAT SHALL I SAY UNTO THEM?

EXODUS 3:13

AND GOD SAID UNTO MOSES, I AM, THAT I AM AND HE SAID, THUS SHALL THOU SAY UNTO THE CHILDREN OF ISRAEL, I AM HATH SENT ME UNTO YOU.

EXODUS 3:14

YE SHALL KEEP MY SABBATHS AND REVERENCE MY SANCTUARY. I AM THE LORD. FOR I WILL HAVE RESPECT UNTO YOU AND MAKE YOU FRUITFUL AND MULTIPLY YOU AND ESTABLISH YOU.

LEVITICUS 26:2,9

THE LORD BLESS THEE, AND KEEP THEE. THE LORD MAKE HIS FACE SHINE UPON THEE AND BE GRACIOUS UNTO THEE. THE LORD LIFT UP HIS COUNTENANCE UPON THEE AND GIVE THEE PEACE.

NUMBERS 6:24,25,26

AND THERE AROSE NOT A PROPHET SINCE IN ISRAEL LIKE UNTO MOSES, WHO THE LORD KNEW FACE TO FACE.

DEUTERONOMY 34:10

MY SHEEP HEAR MY VOICE AND I KNOW THEM AND THEY FOLLOW ME.

JOHN 10:27

HAVING, THEREFORE, OBTAINED HELP OF GOD, I CONTINUE UNTO THIS DAY, WITNESSING, BOTH, TO SMALL AND GREAT SAYING NONE OTHER THINGS THAN THOSE WHICH THE PROPHETS AND MOSES DID SAY SHOULD COME.

ACTS 26;22

AND, LIKEWISE, ALSO THE MEN LEAVING THE NATURAL USE OF THE WOMAN, BURNED IN THEIR LUST ONE TOWARD ANOTHER, MEN WITH MEN WORKING THAT WHICH IS UNSEEMLY AND RECEIVING IN THEMSELVES THAT RECOMPENCE OF THEIR ERROR THAT WHICH WAS MEET.

ROMANS 1:27

WHERE IS THE WISE? WHERE IS THE SCRIBE? WHERE IS THE DISPUTER OF THIS WORLD? HATH NOT GOD MADE FOOLISH THE WISDOM OF THIS WORLD?

1 CORINTHIANS 1:20

MAY HE BE LIKE RAIN COMING DOWN UPON THE FIELDS, LIKE SHOWERS WATERING THE EARTH.

PSALM 72:6

I AM YOUR GOD, I WILL STRENGTHEN YOU AND HELP YOU. I WILL UPHOLD YOU WITH MY RIGHTEOUS RIGHT HAND.

ISAIH 41:10

HOW BEAUTIFUL ARE THY FEET WITH
SHOES, O PRINCE'S DAUGHTER. THE
JOINTS OF THY THIGHS ARE LIKE JEWELS
THE WORK OF THE HANDS OF A CUNNING
WORKMAN. THY NAVEL IS LIKE A ROUND
GOBLET, WHICH WANTETH NOT LIQUOR,
THY BELLY IS LIKE A HEAP OF WHEAT
SET ABOUT WITH LILLIES. THY TWO
BREASTS ARE LIKE TWO YOUNG ROES
THAT ARE TWINS. THY NECK IS A TOWER
OF IVORY, THINE EYES LIKE THE FISH-
POOLS IN HESHBON BY THE GATE OF
BATHRABBIM. THY NOSE IS AS THE TOWER
OF LEBANON, WHICH LOOKETH TOWARD
DAMASCUS. THINE HEAD, UPON THEE,
IS LIKE CARMEL AND THE HAIR OF THINE
HEAD, LIKE PURPLE, THE KING IS HELD
IN THE GALLERIES. HOW FAIR AND HOW
PLEASANT ART THOU, O LOVE FOR DELIGHTS.
THIS, THY STATURE IS LIKE TO A PALM
TREE. I WILL TAKE HOLD OF THE BOUGHS
THEREOF. NOW, ALSO, THY BREASTS SHALL
BE AS CLUSTERS OF THE VINE AND THE
SMELL OF THY NOSE, LIKE APPLES. AND
THE ROOF OF THY MOUTH, LIKE THE BEST
WINE FOR MY BELOVED THAT GOETH DOWN
SWEETLY, CAUSING THE LIPS OF THOSE
THAT ARE ASLEEP TO SPEAK. I AM MY
BELOVED'S AND HIS DESIRE IS TOWARD ME.
COME, MY BELOVED, LET US GO FORTH INTO
THE FIELD, LET US LODGE IN THE VILLAGES.
LET US GET UP EARLY TO THE VINEYARDS.
LET US SEE IF THE VINE FLOURISH,
WHETHER THE TENDER GRAPE APPEAR AND THE
POMEGRANATES BUD FORTH. THEM, WILL I
GIVE THEE MY LOVES. THE MANDRAKES
GIVE A SMELL AND OF OUR GATES ARE ALL
MANNER OF PLEASANT FRUITS, NEW AND OLD
WHICH I HAVE LAID UP FOR THEE, MY
BELOVED. SONG OF SOLOMON 7

THOU SHALT HAVE NO OTHER GODS
BEFORE ME. THOU SHALT NOT MAKE
UNTO THEE ANY GRAVEN IMAGE.
THOU SHALT NOT TAKE THE NAME OF
THE LORD THY GOD IN VAIN, REMEMBER THE SABBATH DAY TO KEEP IT
HOLY. HONOR THY FATHER AND THY
MOTHER. THOU SHALT NOT KILL,
THOU SHALT NOT COMMIT ADULTERY,
THOU SHALT NOT STEAL, THOU SHALT
NOT BEAR FALSE WITNESS THOU SHALT
NOT COVET THY NEIGHBOR'S HOUSE.

EXODUS 20: 3-17

CAST THY BREAD UPON THE WATERS,
FOR THOU SHALT FIND IT AFTER MANY
DAYS. GIVE A PORTION TO SEVEN
AND ALSO TO EIGHT, FOR THOU KNOWEST NOT WHAT EVIL SHALL BE UPON
THE EARTH. IF THE CLOUDS BE FULL
OF RAIN, THEY EMPTY THEMSELVES
UPON THE EARTH AND IF THE TREE
FALL TOWARD THE SOUTH OR TOWARD
THE NORTH, IN THE PLACE WHERE THE
TREE FALLETH, THERE IT SHALL BE.
HE THAT OBSERVETH THE WIND SHALL
NOT SOW, AND HE THAT REGARDTH
THE CLOUDS, SHALL NOT REAP. AS
THOU KNOWEST NOT WHAT IS THE WAY
OF THE SPIRIT,NOR HOW THE BONES
DO GROW IN THE WOMB OF HER THAT
IS WITH CHILD, EVEN SO THOU
KNOWEST NOT THE WORKS OF GOD WHO
MAKETH ALL.

ECCLESIASTES 11:1-5

I WILL LIFT UP MINE EYES UNTO THE HILLS, FROM WHENCE COMETH MY HELP MY HELP COMETH FROM THE LORD, WHICH MADE HEAVEN AND EARTH. HE WILL NOT SUFFER THY FOOT TO BE MOVED, HE THAT KEEPETH THEE WILL NOT SLUMBER, BEHOLD, HE THAT KEEPETH ISRAEL SHALL NEITHER SLUMBER NOR SLEEP. THE LORD IS THY KEEPER, THE LORD IS THY SHADE UPON THY RIGHT HAND. THE SUN SHALL NOT SMITE THEE BY DAY NOR THE MOON BY NIGHT. THE LORD SHALL PRESERVE THEE FROM ALL EVIL, HE SHALL PRESERVE THY SOUL. THE LORD SHALL PRESERVE THY GOING OUT AND THY COMING IN FROM THIS TIME FORTH AND EVEN FOR EVERMORE.

PSALM 121

LORD THOU HAST BEEN OUR DWELLING PLACE IN ALL GENERATIONS, EVEN FROM EVERLASTING TO EVERLASTING, THOU ART GOD.

PSALM 90:1-2

MAKE A JOYFUL NOISE UNTO THE LORD, ALL YE LANDS. SERVE THE LORD WITH GLADNESS, COME BEFORE HIS PRESENCE WITH SINGING. KNOW YE THAT THE LORD, HE IS GOD, IT IS HE THAT HAS MADE US, AND NOT WE OURSELVES, WE ARE HIS PEOPLE, AND THE SHEEP OF HIS PASTURE. ENTER INTO HIS GATES WITH THANKSGIVING AND INTO HIS COURTS WITH PRAISE, BE THANKFUL UNTO HIM AND BLESS HIS NAME. FOR THE LORD IS GOOD, HIS MERCY EN-DURETH TO ALL GENERATIONS.

PSALM 100

THE HEAVENS DECLARE THE GLORY OF GOD AND THE FIRMAMENT SHEWTH HIS HANDIWORK.

PSALM 19:1

HE THAT DWELLETH IN THE SECRET PLACE OF THE MOST HIGH SHALL ABIDE UNDER THE SHADOW OF THE ALMIGHTY. I WILL SAY OF THE LORD, HE IS MY REFUGE AND MY FORTRESS, MY GOD; IN HIM WILL I TRUST. SURELY HE SHALL DELIVER THE FROM THE SNARE OF THE FOWLER AND FROM THE NOISOME PESTI-LENCE. HE SHALL COVER THEE WITH HIS FEATHERS AND UNDER HIS WINGS SHALT THOU TRUST, HIS TRUTH SHALL BE THY SHIELD AND BUCKLER.

PSALM 91: 1-4

NOW THE LORD HAD PREPARED A GREAT FISH TO SWALLOW UP JONAH. AND JONAH WAS IN THE BELLY OF THE FISH THREE DAYS AND THREE NIGHTS.

JONAH 1:17

THEN JONAH PRAYED UNTO THE LORD, HIS GOD OUT OF THE FISH'S BELLY.

AND SAID, I CRIED BY REASON OF MINE AFFLICTION UNTO THE LORD AND HE HEARD ME, OUT OF THE BELLY OF HELL, CRIED, I AND THOU HEARDEST MY VOICE.

FOR THOU HAST CAST ME INTO THE DEEP. IN THE MIDST OF THE SEAS AND THE FLOODS COMPASSED ME ABOUT, ALL THY BILLOWS AND THY WAVES PASSED OVER ME.

THEN I SAID, I AM CAST OUT OF THY SIGHT, YET, I WILL LOOK AGAIN TOWARD THY HOLY TEMPLE.

THE WATERS COMPASSED ME ABOUT, EVEN TO THE SOUL, THE DEPTH CLOSED ME ROUND ABOUT, THE WEEDS WERE WRAPPED ABOUT MY HEAD.

I WENT DOWN TO THE BOTTOMS OF THE MOUNTAINS, THE EARTH WITH HER BARS WAS ABOUT ME FOREVER. YET, HAST THOU BROUGHT UP MY LIFE FROM CORRUPTION, O LORD MY GOD.

JONAH 2:1-6

ZION SPREADETH FORTH HER HANDS AND THERE IS NONE TO COMFORT HER, THE LORD HATH COMMANDED CONCERNING JACOB THAT HIS ADVERSARIES SHOULD BE ROUND ABOUT HIM. JERUSALEM IS AS A MENSTRUOUS WOMAN AMONG THEM.

LAMENTATIONS !:17

THE LORD IS RIGHTEOUS FOR I HAVE REBELLED AGAINST HIS COMMANDMENT, HEAR, I PRAY YOU, ALL PEOPLE AND BEHOLD MY SORROW, MY VIRGINS AND MY YOUNG MEN ARE GONE INTO CAPTIVITY.

LAMENTATIONS 1:18

THIS MONTH SHALL BE UNTO YOU THE BEGINNING OF MONTHS, IT SHALL BE THE FIRST MONTH OF THE YEAR TO YOU.

SPEAK YE UNTO ALL THE CONGREGATION OF ISRAEL, SAYING, IN THE TENTH DAY OF THIS MONTH THEY SHALL TAKE TO THEM, EVERY MAN A LAMB, ACCORDING TO THE HOUSE OF THEIR FATHERS, A LAMB FOR AN HOUSE.

AND IF THE HOUSEHOLD BE TOO LITTLE FOR THE LAMB, LET HIM AND HIS NEIGHBOR NEXT UNTO HIS HOUSE TAKE IT ACCORDING TO THE NUMBER OF THE SOULS, EVERY MAN ACCORDING TO HIS EATING, SHALL MAKE YOUR COUNT FOR THE LAMB.

EXODUS 12:2,3,4

LET THE WORD OF CHRIST DWELL IN YOU RICHLY IN ALL WISDOM, TEACHING AND ADMONISHING ONE ANOTHER IN PSALMS AND HYMNS AND SPIRITUAL SONGS, SINGING WITH GRACE IN YOUR HEARTS TO THE LORD.

AND WHATSOEVER YE DO IN WORD OR DEED, DO ALL IN THE NAME OF THE LORD, JESUS GIVING THANKS TO GOD AND THE FATHER BY HIM.

WIVES, SUBMIT YOURSELVES UNTO YOUR OWN HUSBANDS AS IT IS FIT IN THE LORD.

HUSBANDS, LOVE YOUR WIVES AND BE NOT BITTER AGAINST THEM.

CHILDREN, OBEY YOUR PARENTS IN ALL THINGS, FOR THIS IS WELL PLEASING UNTO THE LORD.

COLOSSIANS 3:16-20

THE ROD OF REPROOF GIVE WISDOM, BUT, A CHILD LEFT TO HIMSELF BRINGETH HIS MOTHER TO SHAME.

PROVERBS 29:15

THE PROVERBS OF SOLOMON. A WISE SON MAKETH A GLAD FATHER, BUT, A FOOLISH SON IS THE HEAVINESS OF HIS MOTHER.

PROVERBS 10:1

"HOUSES GO FROM FATHER TO SON, NOT FROM FATHER TO DAUGHTER."

SENSE AND SENSIBILITY

"IT'S THE MOST WONDERFUL TIME OF THE YEAR."

HOME ALONE 2

"IF WE CAN'T RENEGOTIATE, WE WITHER AND DIE"

TWINS

"DON'T WORRY MAN, EVERYTHING'S GONNA BE ALRIGHT"

THE WEDDING SINGER

"DON'T TALK TO ME ABOUT DESPERATE"

BANDITS

"WHY DON'T YOU SIT DOWN SOMEWHERE AND FOCUS"

BABY BOY

WISDOM HATH BUILDED HER HOUSE, SHE HATH HEWN OUT HER SEVEN PILLARS.

SHE HATH KILLED HER BEASTS, SHE HATH MINGLED HER WINE, SHE HATH, ALSO, FURNISHED HER TABLE.

SHE HATH SENT FORTH HER MAIDENS, SHE CRIETH UPON THE HIGHEST PLACES OF THE CITY.

WHOSO IS SIMPLE, LET HIM TURN IN HITHER, AS FOR HIM THAT WANTETH UNDERSTANDING, SHE SAITH TO HIM.

COME, EAT OF MY BREAD AND DRINK OF THE WINE WHICH I HAVE MINGLED.

FORSAKE THE FOOLISH AND LIVE AND GO IN THE WAY OF UNDERSTANDING.

PROVERBS 9: 1-6

UNTO YOU FIRST GOD, HAVING RAISED UP HIS SON JESUS, SENT HIM TO BLESS YOU, TURNING AWAY EVERY ONE OF YOU FROM HIS INIQUITIES.

ACTS 3:26

LET HIM THAT STOLE, STEAL NO MORE, BUT, RATHER, LET HIM LABOUR, WORKING WITH HIS HANDS, THE THING WHICH IS GOOD TO HIM THAT NEEDETH.

EPHESIANS 4:28

NOW, WE HAVE RECEIVED, NOT THE SPIRIT
OF THE WORLD, BUT, THE SPIRIT WHICH IS OFF
OF GOD, THAT WE MIGHT KNOW THE THINGS
THAT ARE FREELY GIVEN TO US OF GOD.

WHICH THINGS, ALSO, WE SPEAK, NOT IN
THE WORDS WHICH MAN'S WISDOM TEACHETH,
BUT, WHICH THE HOLY GHOST TEACHETH,
COMPARING SPIRITUAL THINGS WITH
SPIRITUAL.

BUT, THE NATURAL MAN RECEIVETH, NOT, THE
THINGS OF THE SPIRIT OF GOD, FOR THEY
ARE FOOLISHNESS UNTO HIM, NEITHER CAN
HE KNOW THEM, BECAUSE THEY ARE SPIRITUALLY
DISCERNED.

1 CORINTHIANS
2:12-14

SET YOUR AFFECTION ON THINGS ABOVE,
NOT ON THINGS OF THE EARTH.

FOR YE ARE DEAD AND YOUR LIFE IS HID
WITH CHRIST IN GOD.

WHEN CHRIST, WHO IS OUR LIFE SHALL
APPEAR, THEN SHALL YE, ALSO, APPEAR
WITH HIM IN GLORY.

COLOSSIANS 3:2-4

AND JESUS SAID, LET HER ALONE, WHY
TROUBLE YE HER? SHE HATH WROUGHT A
GOOD WORK FOR ME.

MARK 14:6

GIVE INSTRUCTION TO A WISE MAN AND HE WILL BE, YET, WISER, TEACH A JUST MAN AND HE WILL INCREASE IN LEARNING.

THE FEAR OF THE LORD IS THE BEGINNING OF WISDOM AND THE KNOWLEDGE OF THE HOLY IS UNDERSTANDING.

FOR BY ME THY DAYS SHALL BE MULTIPLIED AND THE YEARS OF THY LIFE SHALL BE INCREASED.

IF THOU BE WISE, THOU SHALT BE WISE FOR THYSELF, BUT, IF THOU SCORNEST, THOU, ALONE, SHALT BEAR IT.

A FOOLISH WOMAN IS CLAMOROUS, SHE IS SIMPLE AND KNOWETH NOTHING.

FOR SHE SITTETH AT THE DOOR OF HER HOUSE ON A SEAT IN THE HIGH PLACES OF THE CITY.

TO CALL PASSENGERS, WHO GO RIGHT ON THEIR WAYS.

WHOSO IS SIMPLE, LET HIM TURN IN HITHER AND AS FOR HIM THAT WANTETH UNDERSTANDING, SHE SAITH TO HIM.

STOLEN WATERS ARE SWEET AND BREAD EATEN IN SECRET IS PLEASANT.

BUT, HE KNOWETH NOT THAT THE DEAD ARE THERE AND THAT HER GUESTS ARE IN THE DEPTHS OF HELL.

PROVERBS 9:9-18

THIS MAN

THERE WAS A MAN, ONE SENT FROM GOD
WHO CAME TO EARTH ONE DAY
TO MAKE AMENDS FOR ADAM'S SIN
AND SHOW MANKIND THE WAY
THIS MAN, ALTHOUGH, FROM HEAVEN SENT
IS NOT, BUT, GOD, ALONE
OF VIRGIN PURE HE WAS BEGOT
A MAN, IN FLESH AND BONE
HE IS, BOTH, HUMAN AND DEVINE
IN GOD, HE IS THE SON
BUT, IN MAJESTY, THEY'RE EQUAL, FOR
THE FATHER AND HIS ARE ONE
HE CAME TO EARTH IN HUMAN FORM
TO OPEN HEAVEN'S DOOR
AND SUFFERED ALL, THAT WE MIGHT LIVE
IN LOVE, FOR EVER MORE
HIS BACK WAS TORN BY STINGING WHIPS
A CROWN OF THORNS, HE WORE
HIS SHOULDERS SAGGED BENEATH THE WEIGHT
OF THE HEAVY CROSS HE BORE
AND YET, THROUGH ALL HIS AGONY
THAT ENDED IN HIS DEATH
HE UTTERED ONLY WORDS OF LOVE
UNTO HIS DYING BREATH.

MARY'S CALL

THROUGH FORGIVENESS, THE ARMS OF
JESUS LIFT YOU, HIS BLOOD CLEANSES
YOU AND HIS LOVE CHANGES YOU
TURN YOUR HEART TOWARD JESUS
PRAY TO RECEIVE HIM AND HIS
FORGIVENESS, BY FAITH. HE WILL
COME INTO YOUR HEART AND MAKE
ALL THINGS NEW.

THE WORD AMONG US

THE LORD'S PRAYER

OUR FATHER, WHO ART IN HEAVEN
HALLOWED BE THY NAME, THY
KINGDOM COME, THY WILL
BE DONE ON EARTH, AS IT IS IN HEAVEN.

GIVE US THIS DAY, OUR DAILY BREAD
AND FORGIVE US, OUR TRESPASSES
AS WE FORGIVE THOSE WHO TRESPASS
AGAINST US.

AND LEAD US, NOT INTO TEMPTATION,
BUT, DELIVER US FROM EVIL,
FOR THINE IS THE KINGDOM
AND THE POWER AND THE GLORY, FOREVER

AMEN

HOLY BIBLE
KING JAMES VERSION

MAY THE LORD BLESS AND KEEP YOU,
MAY THE LORD MAKE HIS FACE TO
SHINE UPON YOU AND BE GRACIOUS TO YOU.
MAY THE LORD LIFT UP HIS COUNTENANCE
UPON YOU AND GIVE YOU PEACE.

NUMBERS 6:25,26

WITH GOD, ALL THINGS ARE POSSIBLE.

MATTHEW 19:26

JESUS CAME TO PAY A DEBT
HE DID NOT OWE
BECAUSE WE OWED A DEBT
WE COULD NOT PAY

UNKNOWN

GIVE ME A SPIRIT OF THANKFULNESS, LORD
FOR NUMBERLESS BLESSINGS GIVEN
BLESSINGS THAT DAILY COME TO ME
LIKE DEWDROPS FALLING FROM HEAVEN.

DAWE
ODB

I HAVE A FRIEND WHO'S FAITHFUL LOVE
IS MORE THAN ALL THE WORLD TO ME
IT'S HIGHER THAN THE HEIGHTS ABOVE
AND DEEPER THAN THE BOUNDLESS SEA.

ANONYMOUS

TO MOSES AT THE BURNING BUSH
GOD SPOKE HIS NAME, IT WAS I AM
AND JESUS, ALSO, TOOK THAT NAME
I AM, THE SACRIFICIAL LAMB.

HESS
ODB

HELP US NOT TO CLOUD GOD'S GLORY
NOR WITH SELF, HIS LIGHT DIM.
MAY EACH THOUGHT. TO CHRIST BE CAPTIVE
EMPTIED, TO BE FILLED WITH HIM.

ANONYMOUS

THANKS O LORD FOR BOUNDLESS MERCY
FROM THY GRACIOUS THRONE ABOVE
THANKS FOR EVERY NEED PROVIDED
FROM THE FULLNESS OF THY LOVE.

STORM
ODB

SOMETIMES WE SEE A MIRACLE
AND FAITH IN GOD REVIVES
YET, WE SHOULD SEE GOD'S GRACIOUS HAND
AT WORK THROUGHT OUR LIVES.

HESS
ODB

THE ONE WHO MADE THE HEAVENS
WHO DIED ON CALVARY
REJOICES WITH HIS ANGELS
WHEN ONE SOUL IS SET FREE.

FASICK
ODB

I CAN ALWAYS COUNT ON GOD
MY HEAVENLY FATHER
FOR HE ALWAYS IS THE SAME
YESTERDAY, TODAY, FOREVER
HE IS FAITHFUL
AND I KNOW HE LOVES ME
PRAISE HIS HOLY NAME.

FELTON
ODB

WHEN EARTHQUAKES AND CALAMITIES
INCREASINGLY APPEAR
LOOK UP, TRUST GOD, HE'S IN CONTROL
REDEMPTION'S DRAWING NEAR.

HESS
ODB

SURER THAN AUTUMN'S HARVESTS
ARE HARVESTS OF THOUGHT AND DEED
LIKE THOSE THAT OUR HANDS HAVE PLANTED
THE YIELD WILL BE LIKE THE SEED.

HARRIS
ODB

I KNOW NOT WHY GOD'S WONDROUS GRACE
TO ME HE HATH MADE KNOWN
NOR WHY UNWORTHY CHRIST IN LOVE
REDEEMED ME FOR HIS OWN.

WHITTLE
ODB

THE HURTING ONES NEED SYMPATHY
THEY NEED TO KNOW WE'RE THERE
A QUIET WORD, A TENDER TOUCH
ASSURES THEM THAT WE CARE.

DeHAAN
ODB

REACH OUT IN JESUS' NAME
WITH HANDS OF LOVE AND CARE
TO THOSE WHO ARE IN NEED
AND CAUGHT IN LIFE'S DESPAIR.

SPER
ODB

GLORY TO GOD WITH PRAISE AND LOVE
BE EVER, EVER GIVEN
BY SAINTS BELOW AND SAINTS ABOVE
THE CHURCH IN EARTH AND HEAVEN.

WESLEY
ODB

AND SAY UNTO THEM, THUS SAITH THE LORD, GOD. IN THE DAY WHEN I CHOSE ISRAEL AND LIFTED UP MINE HAND UNTO THE SEED OF THE HOUSE OF JACOB AND MADE MYSELF KNOWN UNTO THEM IN THE LAND OF EGYPT WHEN I LIFTED UP MINE HAND UNTO THEM, SAYING, I AM THE LORD YOUR GOD.

EZEKIEL 19:5

AND HE HATH CONFIRMED HIS WORDS WHICH HE SPAKE AGAINST US AND AGAINST OUR JUDGES THAT JUDGED US BY BRINGING UPON US, A GREAT EVIL FOR UNDER THE WHOLE HEAVEN, HATH NOT BEEN DONE AS HATH BEEN DONE UPON JERUSALEM.

DANIEL 9:12

AND BEHOLD, THE WHOLE FAMILY IS RISEN AGAINST THINE HANDMAID AND THEY SAID DELIVER HIM THAT SMOTE HIS BROTHER THAT WE MAY KILL HIM FOR THE LIFE OF HIS BROTHER, WHOM HE SLEW. AND WE WILL DESTROY THE HEIR, ALSO, AND SO THEY SHALL QUENCH MY COAL WHICH IS LEFT AND SHALL NOT LEAVE TO MY HUSBAND, NEITHER NAME NOR REMAINDER UPON THE EARTH.

2 SAMUEL 14:7

AND THE WOMAN SAID TO ELIJAH, NOW BY THIS I KNOW THAT THOU ART A MAN OF GOD AND THAT THE WORD OF THE LORD IN THY MOUTH IS TRUTH.

1 KINGS 17:24

ACCORDING TO THE WORD THAT I COVENANTED WITH YOU WHEN YE CAME OUT OF EGYPT, SO MY SPIRIT REMAINETH AMONG YOU, FEAR YE NOT.

HAGGAI 2:5

AND I WILL BRING THE THIRD PART THRU THE FIRE AND WILL REFINE THEM AS GOLD IS TRIED THEY SHALL CALL ON MY NAME AND I WILL HEAR THEM, I WILL SAY IT IS MY PEOPLE AND THEY SHALL SAY THE LORD IS MY GOD.

ZECHARIAH 13:9

FOR I AM THE LORD, I CHANGE NOT, THEREFORE YE SONS OF JACOB ARE NOT CONSUMED.

MALACHI 3:6

THE LORD IS GOOD, A STRONG HOLD IN THE DAY OF TROUBLE AND HE KNOWETH THEM THAT TRUST IN HIM.

NAHUM 1:7

FOR THE EARTH SHALL BE FILLED WITH THE KNOWLEDGE OF THE GLORY OF THE LORD AS THE WATERS COVER THE SEA.

HABAKKUK 2:14

SHE OBEYED, NOT THE VOICE, SHE RECEIVED NOT CORRECTION, SHE TRUSTED NOT IN THE LORD, SHE DREW NOT NEAR TO HER GOD.

ZEPHANIAH 3:2

NOT BOASTING OF THINGS WITHOUT OUR MEASURE, THAT IS, OF OTHER MEN'S LABOURS, BUT, HAVING HOPE, WHEN YOUR FAITH IS INCREASED THAT WE SHALL BE ENLARGED BY YOU ACCORDING TO OUR RULE, ABUNDANTLY.

2 CORINSTHIANS 10:15

BEAR YE ONE ANOTHER'S BURDENS, AND SO FULFILL THE LAW OF CHRIST.

GALATIANS 6:2

GIVING THANKS ALWAYS FOR ALL THINGS UNTO GOD AND THE FATHER IN THE NAME OF OUR LORD JESUS CHRIST.

EPHESIANS 5:20

BE CAREFUL FOR NOTHING, BUT, IN EVERYTHING BY PRAYER AND SUPPLICATION WITH THANKSGIVING, LET YOUR REQUESTS BE MADE KNOWN TO GOD.

PHILIPPIANS 4:6

SET YOUR AFFECTION ON THINGS ABOVE, NOT ON THINGS ON THE EARTH.

COLOSSIANS 3:2

IN EVERYTHING, GIVE THANKS FOR THIS IS THE WILL OF GOD IN CHRIST JESUS, CONCERNING YOU.

1 THESSALONIANS 5:15

THOUGH I SPEAK WITH THE TONGUES OF ANGELS AND HAVE NOT CHARITY, I AM BECOME AS A SOUNDING BRASS, OR A TINKLING CYMBAL. AND THOUGH I HAVE THE GIFT OF PROPHECY AND UNDERSTAND ALL MYSTERIES AND ALL KNOWLEDGE AND THOUGH I HAVE ALL FAITH, SO THAT I COULD REMOVE MOUNTAINS AND HAVE NOT CHARITY, I AM NOTHING.

AND THOUGH I BESTOW ALL MY GOODS TO FEED THE POOR AND THOUGH I GIVE MY BODY TO BE BURNED AND HAVE NOT CHARITY, I AM NOTHING.

CHARITY SUFFERETH LONG AND IS KIND, CHARITY ENVIETH NOT, CHARITY VAUNTETH NOT ITSELF, IS NOT PUFFED UP. DOETH NOT BEHAVE ITSELF UN-SEEMLY, SEEKETH NOT HER OWN IS NOT EASILY PROVOKED, THINKETH NO EVIL.

REJOICE NOT IN INIQUITY, BUT, RE-JOICETH IN THE TRUTH. BEAR ALL THINGS, BELIEVETH ALL THINGS HOPETH ALL THINGS, ENDURETH ALL THINGS.

1 CORINTHIANS 13: 1-7

AND KING SOLOMON SHALL BE BLESSED AND THE THRONE OF DAVID SHALL BE ESTABLISHED BEFORE THE LORD FOREVER.

1 KINGS 2:45

THOUGH I SPEAK WITH THE TONGUES OF
MEN AND OF ANGELS AND HAVE NOT CHARITY
I AM BECOME AS SOUNDING BRASS OR A
TINKLING CYMBAL. AND THOUGH I HAVE
THE GIFT OF PROPHECY AND UNDERSTAND
ALL MYSTERIES AND ALL KNOWLEDGE AND
THOUGH I HAVE ALL FAITH, SO THAT I
COULD REMOVE MOUNTAINS AND HAVE NOT
CHARITY, I AM NOTHING. AND THOUGH
I BESTOW ALL MY GOODS TO FEED THE
POOR AND THOUGH I GIVE MY BODY TO BE
BURNED AND HAVE NOT CHARITY, I AM
NOTHING. CHARITY SUFFERETH LONG AND
IS KIND, CHARITY ENVIETH NOT, CHARITY
VAUNTETH NOT ITSELF, IS NOT PUFFED UP
DOETH NOT BEHAVE ITSELF UNSEEMLY,
SEEKETH NOT HER OWN, IS NOT EASILY
PROVOKED, THINKETH NO EVIL, REJOICETH
NOTIN INIQUITY, BUT, REJOICETH IN THE
TRUTH. BEARETH ALL THINGS, BELIEVETH
ALL THINGS, HOPETH ALL THINGS, EN-
DURETH ALL THINGS.

1CORINTHIANS 13:1-7

HE THAT SPARETH HIS ROD, HATETH HIS
SON, BUT, HE THAT LOVETH, CHASTENETH
HIM BETIMES.

PROVERBS 13: 24

I OPENED TO MY BELOVED, BUT MY BELOVED
HAD WITHDRAWN HIMSELF AND WAS GONE,
MY SOUL FAILED WHEN HE SPAKE, I
SOUGHT HIM, BUT, I COULD NOT FIND HIM,
I CALLED HIM, BUT, HE GAVE ME NO ANSWER

SONG OF SOLOMON 5:6

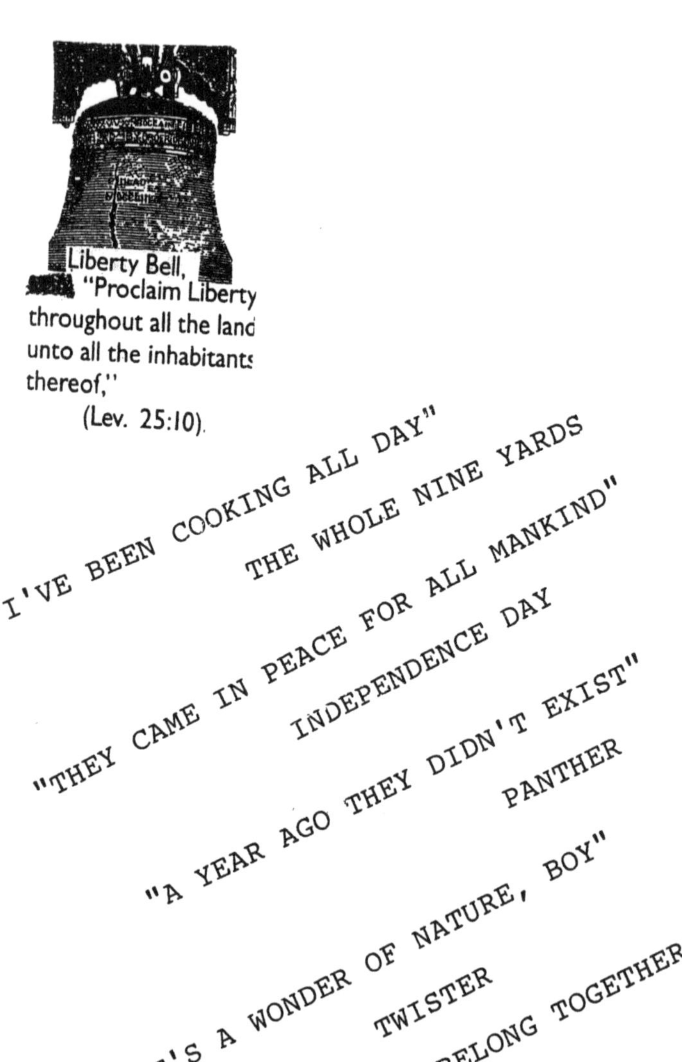

"I'VE BEEN COOKING ALL DAY"
THE WHOLE NINE YARDS

"THEY CAME IN PEACE FOR ALL MANKIND"
INDEPENDENCE DAY

"A YEAR AGO THEY DIDN'T EXIST"
PANTHER

"IT'S A WONDER OF NATURE, BOY"
TWISTER

"YOU'RE MINE AND WE BELONG TOGETHER"
SELENA

LET THE HEAVENS REJOICE AND LET THE EARTH BE GLAD, LET THE SEA ROAR AND THE FULLNESS THEREOF, LET THE FIELD BE JOYFUL AND ALL THAT IS THEREIN, THEN SHALL ALL THE TREES OF THE WOOD REJOICE BEFORE THE LORD, FOR HE COMETH TO JUDGE THE EARTH, HE SHALL JUDGE THE WORLD WITH RIGHTEOUSNESS AND THE PEOPLE WITH HIS TRUTH.

PSALM 96:11-13

ASK AND IT SHALL BE GIVEN YOU, SEEK AND YE SHALL FIND, KNOCK AND IT SHALL BE OPENED OR WHAT MAN IS THERE OF YOU, WHOM IF, HIS SON ASK BREAD, WILL HE GIVE HIM A STONE? OR IF HE ASK A FISH, WILL HE GIVE HIM A SERPENT? IF YE THEN, BEING EVIL KNOW HOW TO GIVE GOOD GIFTS UNTO YOUR CHILDREN, HOW MUCH MORE SHALL YOUR FATHER, WHICH IS IN HEAVEN, GIVE GOOD THINGS TO THEM THAT ASK HIM?

MATTHEW 7:7; 9-11

THOU HAST GRANTED ME LIFE AND FAVOUR
AND THY VISITATION HATH PRESERVED
MY SPIRIT.

JOB 10:12

BE NOT A WITNESS AGAINST THY NEIGHBOR
WITHOUT CAUSE AND DECEIVE NOT WITH
THY LIPS.

PROVERBS 24:28

MANY WATERS CANNOT QUENCH LOVE,
NEITHER CAN THE FLOODS DOWN IT. IF
A MAN WOULD GIVE ALL THE SUBSTANCE OF
HIS HOUSE FOR LOVE, IT WOULD UTTERLY
BE CONTEMNED.

SONG OF SOLOMON 8:7

I KNOW WHAT IT IS TO BE LOVED
I KNOW WHAT IT IS TO BE IN LOVE,
I KNOW WHAT IT IS TO LOVE
BUT, MOST OF ALL, I KNOW WHAT LOVE IS.

EMD

I AM THE AUTHOR OF THE ONLY DICTIONARY
THAT DEFINES ME.

STAR JONES
"STAR JONES FOR
THE PEOPLE"

AND AS THE KING OF ISRAEL WAS PASSING BY UPON THE WALL THERE CRIED A WOMAN UNTO HIM, SAYING, HELP, MY LORD O KING.

2 KINGS 6:26

AND SATAN STOOD UP AGAINST ISRAEL AND PROVOKED DAVID TO NUMBER ISRAEL.

1 CHRONICLES 21:1

THAT WHOSOEVER WOULD NOT SEEK THE LORD GOD OF ISRAEL, WHETHER SMALL OR GREAT, WHETHER MAN OR WOMAN.

2 CHRONICLES 15:13

GIVE YE, NOW COMMANDMENTS TO CAUSE THESE MEN TO CEASE AND THAT THE CITY BE NOT BUILDED UNTIL COMMANDMENT SHALL BE GIVEN FROM ME.

EZRA 4:21

AND DIDST see the affliction of our FATHERS IN EGYPT AND HEARDEST THEIR CRY BY THE RED SEA.

NEHEMIAH 9:9

THEN ESTHER, THE QUEEN, ANSWERED AND SAID IF I HAVE FOUND FAVOUR IN THY SIGHT O KING AND IF IT PLEASE THE KING, LET MY LIFE BE GIVEN ME AT MY PETITION AND MY PEOPLE AT MY REQUEST.

ESTHER 7:3

AND SHOULD NOT I SPARE NINEVEH, THE GREAT CITY, WHEREIN ARE MORE THAN SIXSCORE THOUSAND PERSONS THAT CANNOT DISCERN BETWEEN THEIR RIGHT HAND AND THEIR LEFT HAND AND ALSO MUCH CATTLE.

JONAH 4:11

HEAR, ALL YE PEOPLE, HEARKEN O EARTH AND ALL THAT THEREIN IS AND LET THE LORD GOD BE WITNESS AGAINST YOU, THE LORD FROM HIS HOLY TEMPLE.

MICAH 1:2

THE WOMEN OF MY PEOPLE HAVE YE CAST OUT FROM THEIR PLEASANT HOUSES, FROM THEIR CHILDREN HAVE YE TAKEN AWAY MY GLORY FOR EVER.

MICAH 2:9

COME YE NEAR UNTO ME, HEAR YE THIS, I HAVE NOT SPOKEN IN SECRET FROM THE BEGINNING, FROM THE THE TIME THAT IT WAS, THERE AM I AND NOW THE LORD GOD, AND HIS SPIRIT HATH SENT ME.

THUS SAITH THE LORD, THY REDEEMER, THE HOLY ONE OF ISRAEL. I AM THE LORD THY GOD WHICH TEACHETH THEE TO PROFIT, WHICH LEADETH THEE BY THE WAY THAT SHOULDEST GO.

ISAIAH 48:16,17

AND O'NAN KNEW THAT THE SEED SHOULD NOT BE HIS AND IT CAME TO PASS, WHEN HE WENT IN UNTO HIS BROTHER'S WIFE, THAT HE SPILLED IT ON THE GROUND LEST THAT HE SHOULD GIVE SEED TO HIS BROTHER.

GENESIS 38:9

AND JOSEPH WAS BROUGHT DOWN TO EGYPT AND POTIPHAR, AN OFFICER OF PHARAOH, CAPTAIN OF THE GUARD, AN EGYPTIAN, BOUGHT HIM OF THE HANDS OF THE ISH-MEELITES, WHICH HAD BROUGHT HIM DOWN THITHER.

GENESIS 39:1

AND THE FIELDS SHALL BE BOUGHT IN THIS LAND, WHEREOF YE SAY, IT IS DE-DOLATE WITHOUT MAN OR BEAST. IT IS GIVEN INTO THE HAND OS THE CHALDEANS.

JEREMIAH 32:43

THEN CAME THE WORD OF THE LORD UNTO JEREMIAH, SAYING BEHOLD I AM THE LORD THE GOD OF ALL FLESH. IS THERE ANY THING TOO HARD FOR ME?

JEREMIAH 32:26,27

SHE WEEPETH SORE IN THE NIGHT AND HER TEARS ARE ON HER CHEEKS, AMONG ALL HER LOVERS SHE HATH NONE TO COM-FORT HER. ALL HER FRIENDS HAVE DEALT TREACHEROUSLY WITH HER, THEY ARE BE-COME HER ENEMIES.

LAMENTATIONS 1:2

AND GOD HEARD THEIR GROANING AND GOD REMEMBERED HIS COVENANT WITH ABRAHAM, WITH ISAAC AND WITH JACOB.

EXODUS 2:24

NOT BY WORKS OF RIGHTEOUSNESS WHICH WE HAVE DONE, BUT, ACCORDING TO HIS MERCY, HE SAVED US, BY THE WASHING OF REGENERATION AND RENEWING OF THE HOLY GHOST.

TITUS 3:5

NOT NOW AS A SERVANT, BUT, ABOVE A SERVANT, A BROTHER, BELOVED, SPECIALLY TO ME, BUT, HOW MUCH MORE UNTO THEE, BOTH IN THE FLESH AND IN THE LORD.

PHILEMON 1:16

REMEMBER THEM WHICH HAVE RULE OVER YOU, WHO HAVE SPOKEN UNTO YOU, THE WORD OF GOD, WHOSE FAITH FOLLOW, CONSIDERING THE END OF THEIR CONVERSATION.

HEBREWS 13:7

AND HE PRAYED AGAIN AND THE HEAVEN GAVE RAIN AND THE EARTH BROUGHT FORTH HER FRUIT.

JAMES 5:18

FOR ALL FLESH IS AS GRASS, AND ALL THE GLORY OF MAN AS THE FLOWER OF GRASS. THE GRASS WITHERETH AND THE FLOWER,THEREOF, FALLETH AWAY.

1 PETER 1:24

FOR THE LORD OUR GOD, HE IT IS THAT BROUGHT US UP AND OUR FATHERS OUT OF THE LAND OF EGYPT FROM THE HOUSE OF BONDAGE AND WHICH DID THOSE GREAT SIGNS IN OUR SIGHT AND PRESERVED US IN ALL THE WAY WHEREIN WE WENT AND AMONG ALL THE PEOPLE THROUGH WHOM WE PASSED.

JOSHUA 24:17

AND SHE MADE HIM SLEEP UPON HER KNEES AND SHE CALLED FOR A MAN AND SHE CAUSED HIM TO SHAVE OFF THE SEVEN LOCKS OF HIS HEAD AND SHE BEGAN TO AFFLICT HIM AND HIS STRENGTH LEFT HIM.

JUDGES 16:19

AND RUTH SAID, INTREAT ME NOT TO LEAVE THEE, OR TO RETURN FROM FOLLOWINS AFTER THEE; FOR WHITHER THOU GOEST, I WILL GO AND WHERE THOU LODGEST I WILL LODGE, THY PEOPLE SHALL BE MY PEOPLE AND THY GOD MY GOD.

RUTH 1:6

HE RAISETH UP THE POOR OUT OF THE DUST AND LIFTETH UP THE BEGGAR FROM THE DUNG HILL TO SET THEM AMONG PRINCES AND TO MAKE THEM INHERIT THE THRONE OF GLORY. FOR THE PILLARS OF THE EARTH ARE THE LORD'S AND HE HATH SET THE WORLD UPON THEM.

1 SAMUEL 2:8

FOR THE CREATURE WAS MADE SUBJECT TO VANITY, NOT WILLINGLY, BUT, BY REASON OF HIM WHO HATH SUBJECTED THE SAME TO HOPE.

ROMANS 8: 20

FOR GOD, SO LOVED THE WORLD THAT HE GAVE HIS ONLY BEGOTTEN SON THAT WHO SO EVER BELIEVETH IN HIM SHOULD NOT PERISH BUT HAVE EVERLASTING LIVE.

JOHN 3: 16

FOR IF YE LIVE AFTER THE FLESH, YE SHALL DIE BUT, IF YE THROUGH THE SPIRIT DO MORTIFY THE DEEDS OF THE BODY, YE SHALL LIVE.

ROMANS 8: 13

FOR YE HAVE NOT RECEIVED THE SPIRIT OF BONDAGE AGAIN TO FEAR, BUT, YE HAVE RECEIVED THE SPIRIT OF ADOPTION WHEREBY WE CRY, ABBA FATHER.

ROMANS 8: 15

LITTLE CHILDREN, KEEP YOURSELVES FROM IDOLS. AMEN.

1 JOHN 5: 21

NO MAN HATH SEEN GOD AT ANY TIME. IF WE LOVE ONE ANOTHER GOD DWELLETH IN US, AND HIS LOVE IS PERFECTED IN US.

1 JOHN 4: 12

HEREBY, KNOW YE THE SPIRIT OF GOD. EVERY SPIRIT THAT CONFESSETH THAT JESUS CHRIST IS COME IN THE FLESH IS OF GOD.

1 JOHN 4: 2

YE ARE OF GOD LITTLE CHILDREN AND HAVE OVERCOME THEM BECAUSE GREATER IS HE THAT IS IN US THAN HE THAT IS IN THE WORLD.

WE ARE OF GOD, HE THAT KNOWETH GOD HEARTH US, HE THAT IS NOT OF GOD HEARETH NOT US. HEREBY KNOW WE THE SPIRIT OF TRUTH AND THE SPIRIT OF ERROR.

1 JOHN 4: 4,6

BELOVED, LET US LOVE ONE ANOTHER FOR LOVE IS OF GOD AND ONE THAT LOVETH IS BORN OF GOD AND KNOWETH GOD. HE THAT LOVETH NOT KNOWETH NOT GOD, FOR GOD IS LOVE.

1 JOHN 4: 7,8

IN this was manifested the love of god toward us because that god sent his only BEGOTTEN SON INTO THE WORLD THAT WE MIGHT LIVE THROUGH HIM.

1 JOHN 4: 9

HEREIN IS LOVE, NOT THAT WE LOVED GOD, BUT, THAT HE LOVED US AND SENT HIS SON TO BE THE PROPITIATION FOR OUR SINS.

1 JOHN 4: 10

AND MOUNT SIANI WAS ALTOGETHER ON A SMOKE BECAUSE THE LORD DECENDED UPON IT IN FIRE AND THE SMOKE THEREOF ASCENDED AS THE SMOKE OF A FURNACE AND THE WHOLE MOUNT QUAKED GREATLY.

EXODUS 19: 18

WHOSE VOICE THEN SHOOK THE EARTH, BUT, NOW HE HATH PROMISED SAYING YET ONCE MORE I SHAKE NOT THE EARTH ONLY BUT, ALSO, HEAVEN.

HEBREWS 12: 26

AND TO JESUS THE MEDIATOR OF THE NEW COVENANT AND TO THE BLOOD OF SPRINKLING THAT SPEAKETH BETTER THINGS THAN THAT OF ABEL.

HEBREWS 12: 24

FOR YE ARE NOT COME UNTO THE MOUNT HE TOUCHED AND THAT BURNED WITH FIRE NOR UNTO BLACKNESS AND DARKNESS AND TEMPEST.

HEBREWS 12: 18

BUT, YE ARE COME UNTO MOUNT SION AND UNTO THE CITY OF THE LIVING GOD, THE HEAVENLY JERSALEM AND TO AN INNUMERABLE COMPANY OF ANGELS.

HEBREWS 12:22

IF A MAN SAY I LOVE GOD AND HATETH HIS BROTHER HE IS A LIAR FOR HE THAT LOVETH NOT HIS BROTHER WHOM HE HATH SEEN HOW CAN HE LOVE GOD WHOM HE HATH NOT SEEN?

AND THIS COMMANDMENT HAVE WE FROM HIM, THAT HE WHO LOVETH GOD LOVE HIS BROTHER, ALSO.

1 JOHN 4: 20,21

LET BROTHERLY LOVE CONTINUE.

HEBREWS 13: 4

LET YOUR CONVERSATION BE WITHOUT COVETOUSNESS AND BE CONTENT WITH SUCH THINGS AS YE HAVE FOR HE HATH SAID, I WILL NEVER LEAVE THEE NOR FORSAKE THEE. SO THAT WE MAY BOLDLY SAY THE LORD IS MY HELPER AND I WILL NOT FEAR WHAT MAN SHALL DO UNTO ME.

HEBREWS 13: 5,6

JESUS CHRIST IS THE SAME YESTERDAY AND TODAY AND FOR ERER.

HEBREWS 13: 8

NOW, THE GOD OF PEACE THAT BROUGHT AGAIN FROM THE DEAD OUR LORD JESUS, THAT GREAT SHEPHERD OF SHEEP THROUGH THE BLOOD OF THE EVERLASTING COVENANT.

HEBREWS 13: 20

TO THE GENERAL ASSEMBLY AND CHURCH OF THE FIRSTBORN WHICH ARE WRITTEN IN HEAVEN AND TO GOD THE JUDGE OF ALL AND TO THE SPIRITS OF JUST MEN MADE PERFECT.

HEBREWS 12: 23

WHEREFORE, SEEING WE, ALSO, ARE COMPASSED ABOUT WITH SO GREAT A CLOUD OF WITNESSES LET US LAY ASIDE EVERY WEIGHT AND THE SIN WHICH DOTH SO EASILY BESET US AND RUN WITH PATIENCE, THE RACE THAT IS SET BEFORE US.

HEBREWS 12: 1,2

AND WE KNOW THAT ALL THINGS WORK TOGETHER FOR GOOD TO THEM THAT LOVE GOD TO THEM WHO ARE THE CALLED ACCORDING TO HIS PURPOSE.

ROMANS 8: 28

****

ONCE IN A LIFETIME

TWO PATHS CROSS
LIKE A COMET IN FLIGHT
NEVER PAUSING TO WONDER
IF LIFE MATTERS AT ALL

TWO SOULS MEET
LIKE TWILIGHT'S LAST GLEAM
NEVER STOPPING TO THINK
IF LOVE CAN BE EVERYTHING

TWO LIVES TOUCH
LIKE TRAINS IN THE NIGHT
NEVER WAITING FOR A SIGNAL
THAT MIGHT RIGHT A WRONG

TWO HEARTS COLLIDE
LIKE BROKEN PIECES OF GLASS
NEVER LOOKING BACK
TO CARE, NOT AT ALL.

EMD

HEAR THE VOICE OF GOD

THE VOICE OF GOD IS HEARD WHEN YOU CAN IMAGINE A BABY BIRD, LEAVING IT'S NEST FOR THE VERY FIRST TIME.

THE LEGS ARE THE TINIEST, THE FEET, THE SMALLEST, THE WINGS CAN BARELY FLAP, THE EYES CAN SLOWLY SEE, THE HEAD, HELD UNSTEADY

WHEN THE FLAP OF IT'S WING, THE TAP OF IT'S FEET, THE WINK OF IT'S EYES, THE WOBBLE OF IT'S LEGS, THE CHIRP, CHIRP FROM IT'S MOUTH IS COMPLETELY STILL, EVER SO QUIET, THEN YOU CAN HEAR THE VOICE OF GOD.

EMD

I FEEL LIKE A COMPLETE IDIOT.

COMING TO AMERICA

"ANTICIPATION DENOTES INTELLIGENCE"

THE FIFTH ELEMENT

"DO YOU HAVE THE SLIGHTEST IDEA WHAT A MORAL AND ETHICAL IDEA IS?"

THE SHINING

"BEAUTY AND BRAINS ARE SOMETHING TO DIE FOR"

DEAD BY SUNSET

"AGNOS, WHO DID THIS TO YOU?"

AGNOS OF GOD

MEMORIAL AFTERWORDS

MOTHER TERESA WAS A SPIRIT THAT TOUCHED THE SPIRITS OF OTHERS IN WAYS THAT THOSE OF ORGANIZED GROUPS COULD NEVER DO. HERS WAS A DETERMINED MISSION, SO FOCUSED, THAT ALL AREAS OF THE WORLD WOULD MISS IN HER PASSING.

MRS. PARKS CAN REST KNOWING THAT HER CHALLENGE OF FALSE AUTHORITY WAS NOT IN VAIN. LIKE ANYTHING OF WORTH, IT WOULD TAKE TOIL AND TIME, BUT, HER EFFORTS WERE REWARDED WHEN A MALE CAUCASIAN BUS PASSENGER, NOT ONLY YIELDED HIS SEAT TO ME IN FRONT OF THE BUS, BUT, LEFT AN ABRAHAM LINCOLN FIVE DOLLAR BILL IN THE SEAT IN CASE I WAS SHORT OF FARE. TIMES CHANGE AND SO DO PEOPLE.

MRS. KING MAY HAVE LEFT US AFTER A RELATIVELY SHORT LIFETIME, BUT, HER REWARDS FOR HER CONTRIBUTIONS WILL BE FELT BY MANY FOR A LONG TIME TO COME. HERS WAS EFFORTS TO HELP US UNDERSTAND THAT A TRUE ATTITUDE OF NON-VIOLENCE BEGINS IN THE HEART TO CHANGE ALL PEOPLE.

A MEMORIAL TRIBUTE TO THREE WELL-KNOWN AND COURAGEOUS WOMEN OF OUR TIME.
MOTHER TERESA
ROSA PARKS
CORETTA SCOTT-KING

EMD

MEMORIAL AFTERWORDS (CON'D)

THE WORD 'SUPREME' WOULD NOT HAVE REAL MEANING IN MODERN TIMES IF WE HAD NOT HAD FORMER CHIEF JUSTICE WILLIAM RHEINQUEST TO PERFORM SUCH LASTING EVENTS AS THE SWEARING IN OF MEN FILLING THE OFFICE OF UNITED STATES PRESIDENT. THIS, ALONE, IS WORTHY OF REMEMBERANCE.

JOHN JOHNSON WAS A MAN OF VISION AND DREAMS. BOTH, OF WHICH WILL CONTINUE TO SHOW HIM THE DEDICATED AND DETERMINED LEADER AND BUSINESSMAN THAT HE WAS. READING, WRITING AND RHETORIC WOULD NOT BE WHAT IT IS TODAY WITHOUT THE COMING OF THE WORLDWIDE FAMILY OF JOHN PUBLISHING COMPANY.

LIFE WOULD NOT BE BEARABLE FOR MANY WITHOUT A SENSE OF HUMOR. A CAPACITY FOR JOY IS GOD-GIVEN TO ALL. AND JOHNNY CARSON CONTRIBUTED SO MUCH TO THIS HUMOR AND JOY THAT IT GOES WITHOUT SAYING THAT HE IS SURELY MISSED BY MANY.

A MEMORIAL TRIBUTE TO THREE WELL-KNOWN AND COURAGEOUS MEN OF OUR TIME.
U.S. SUPREME COURT JUSTICE WMN.RHEINQUEST
JOHN JOHNSON
JOHNNY CARSON

EMD

My son, if thou wilt
receive My words and hide
My Commandments with thee
So that thou incline thine
ear unto wisdom and apply
thine heart to understanding
yea if thou criest after
Knowledge and liftest
up thy voice for understanding
If thou seekest her as
for hid treasures,
Then shalt thou under-
stand the fear of the
Lord, and find the know-
ledge of God.

Proverbs 2:1-5

OLD TESTAMENT

GENESIS
EXODUS
LEVITICUS
NUMBERS
DEUTERONOMY
JOSHUA
JUDGES
RUTH
1 SAMUEL
2 SAMUEL
1 KINGS
2 KINGS
1 CHRONICLES
2 CHRONICLES
EZRA
NEHEMIAH
ESTHER
JOB
PSALMS
PROVERBS
ECCLESIASTES
SONG OF SOLOMON
ISAIAH
JEREMIAH
LAMENTATIONS
EZEKIEL
DAIIEL
HOSEA
JOEL
AMOS
OBADIAH
JONAH
MICAH
NAHUM
HABAKKUK
ZEPHANIAH
HAGGAI
ZECHARIAH
MALACHI

NEW TESTAMENT

MATTHEW
MARK
LUKE
JOHN
ACTS
ROMANS
1 CORINTHIANS
2 CORINTHIANS
GALATIANS
EPHESIANS
PHILIPPIANS
COLOSSIANS
1 THESSALONIANS
2 THESSALONIANS
1 TIMOTHY
2 TIMOTHY
TITUS
PHILEMON
HEBREWS
JAMES
1 PETER
2 PETER
1 JOHN
2 JOHN
3 JOHN
JUDE
REVELATION

PRESIDENTS OF THE UNITED STATES

GEORGE WASHINGTON
JOHN ADAMS
THOMAS JEFFERSON
JAMES MADISON
JAMES MONROE
JOHN QUINCY ADAMS
ANDREW JACKSON
MARTIN VAN BUREN
WILLIAM HENRY HARRISON
JOHN TYLER
JAMES KNOX POLK
ZACHARY TAYLOR
MILLARD FILMORE
FRANKLIN PIERCE
JAMES BUCHANAN
ABRAHAM LINCOLN
ANDREW JOHNSON
ULYSSES SIMPSON GRANT
RUTHERFORD BIRCHARD HAYES
JAMES ABRAM GARFIELD
CHESTER ALAN ARTHUR
STHEPHEN GROVER CLEVELAND
BENJAMIN HARRISON
WILLIAM McKINLEY
THEODORE ROOSEVELT
WILLIAM HOWARD TAFT
THOMAS WOODROW WILSON
WARREN GAMALIEL HÀRDING
JOHN CALVIN COOLIDGE
HERBERT CLARK HOOVER
FRANKLIN DELANO ROOSEVELT
HARRY S. TRUMAN
DWIGHT DAVID EISENHOWER
JOHN FITZGERALD KENNEDY
LYNDON BAINES JOHNSON
RICHARD MILHOUSE NIXON
GERALD RUDOLPH FORD
JAMES EARL CARTER
RONALD WILSON REAGAN
GEORGE HERBERT WALKER BUSH
WILLIAM JEFFERSON CLINTON
GEORGE WALKER BUSH

FIRST LADIES
MARTHA
ABIGAIL
MARTHA
DOLLY
ELIZABETH
LOUISA
EMILY
ANGELICA
ANNA
PRISCELLA
SARAH
BETTY
ABIGAIL
JANE
HARRIET
MARY
MARTHA
JULIA
LUCY
LUCRETIA
MARA
FRANCES
CAROLINE
IDA
EDITH
HELEN
EILEN
FLORENCE
GRACE
LOU
ANNA
ELIZABETH
MARIE
JACQULINE
CLAUDIA
THELMA
ELIZABETH
ELENOR
NANCY
BARBARA
HILLARY
LAURA

THE 50 STATES

ALASKA AK
ALABAMA AL
ARKANSAS AR
ARIZONA AZ
CALIFORNIA CA
COLORADO CO
CONNECTICUTT CT
DELAWARE DE
FLORIDA FL
GEORGIA GA
HAWAAI HI
IOWA IA
IDAHO ID
ILLINOIS IL
INDIANA IN
KANSAS KS
KENTUCKY KY
LOUISIANA LA
MASSACHUSETTS MA
MARYLAND MD
MAINE ME
MICHIGAN MI
MINNESOTA MN
MISSOURI MO
MISSISSIPPI MS
MONTANA MT
NORTH CAROLINA NC
NORTH DAKOTA ND
NEBRASKA NE
NEW HAMPSHIRE NH
NEW JERSEY NJ
NEW MEXICO NM
NEVADA NV
NEW YORK NY
OHIO OH
OKLAHOMA OK
OREGON OR
PENNSYLVANIA PA
RHODE ISLAND RI
SOUTH CAROLINA SC
SOUTH DAKOTA SD
TENNESSEE TN
TEXAS TX
UTAH UT
VIRGINIA VA
VERMONT VT
WASHINGTON WA
WISCONSIN WI
WEST VIRGINIA WV
WYOMING WY

EIGHT PARTS OF SPEECH

ADJECTIVE
ADVERB
CONJUNCTION
INTERJECTION
NOUN
PREPOSITION
PRONOUN
VERB

SUPERCALIFRAGILISTICEXPIALIDOCIOUSNESS

VOWELS

A
E
I
O
U

CONSONANTS

B V
C W
D X
F Y
G Z
H
J
K
L
M
N
P
Q
R
S
T

1
2
3
4
5
6
7
8
9
0
1
2
3
4
5
6
7
8
9
0
1
2
3
4
5
6
7
8
9
0

NOTES

Thank
You

AFTERWORDS

IT IS APRIL 18, 2006. IT IS THREE HUNDRED MILES FROM NEW ORLEANS, THE SUBJECT OF THE LOUISIANA PURCHASE, THE LEWIS AND CLARK EXPEDITION AND THE MEMORIBLE 15 MILLION DOLLAR DEAL.

IT IS APRIL 18, 2006. IT IS THREE MORE YEARS LEFT TO GO OF GEORGE BUSH'S DYNASTY (DIE-NASTY), AS WE WONDER HOW MANY OF US WILL BE AROUND TO SEE WHO WILL BE ELECTED TO TRY TO PICK UP THE PIECES AND ONCE AGAIN, ALLOW FOR A NORMAL FOUR YEAR TENURE OF "WHITE HOUSE" CONTROL.

IT IS APRIL 18, 2006 AND I KNOW THAT IF THIS LITERARY EVENT WAS A MONOLOGUE OR A DIALOGUE AND NOT A TRILOGY IN THREE ACTS, THE SUBSTANCE WOULD BE THE SAME.

IF WE WERE IN A COURTROOM, READERS WOULD EXPECT A SUMMATION IN ORDER. BUT, THIS IS NOT A COURTROOM, IT IS SIMPLY THE RECESSES OF MY MIND, THE SHADOWS OF MY EMOTIONS AND THE REALITIES OF MY HEART.

IT IS A TIME WHEN I, PERSONALLY, REMEMBER THE ASSASSINATION OF JOHN KENNEDY AND I COMPARE IT TO THE DESTRUCTION (OR CONSTRUCTION) OF SEPTEMBER 11. IT IS A TIME WHEN I THINK OF THE LOSS (OR GAIN) OF HURRICANE KATRINA.

IT IS A TIME WHEN I FEEL SURE THAT THERE IS A DIFFERENCE IN A MISTAKE AND AN ERROR.

(OVER)

IT'S HUMAN TO ERROR AND AT SOME POINT, ALL THE TRAGEDIES SHOW THIS, THEY ALL HAVE THIS IN COMMON. BUT, I FAIL TO SEE OUR GOVERNMENT. LOCAL, FEDERAL OR WORLD, IGNORANT OF THIS, ALSO. I FAIL TO SEE THAT THEY DON'T AGREE THAT THE OCCURANCES WERE NOT MISTAKES. THAT PART OF GOVERNMENTAL DECISIONS WOULD INVOLVE CHOOSING THE LESSER OF TWO EVILS IN, BOTH, PEACE TIME AND EVEN MORE WHERE THERE ARE THREATS OF WAR. BUT, IT IS ALSO A TIME WHEN I AM WELL AWARE THAT MANY PLAIN EVERYDAY, COMMON FOLK, PRETTY MUCH LIKE MYSELF, FEEL THE REAL QUESTIONS TO PONDER WERE NOT RELATED TO THE MASS OR EN-MASS TRAGEDIES, BUT, TO SIMPLE INCIDENTS, SUCH AS THOSE THAT WOULD INVOLVE THE FATE OF ONE INDIVIDUAL AS IT WOULD BE IN CAPITAL PUNISHMENT IN THIS COUNTRY. WHY DID WE ELECT A PRESIDENT FROM A STATE WEARING A LABEL THAT SPORTS A RECORD FOR THE NUMBER OF CAPITAL PUNISHMENTS ALLOWED? WHY DID WE ELECT A PRESIDENT FROM A STATE WHERE THE MINDS OF SOME INDIVIDUALS ARE SO DEGENERATIVE THAT THEY COME UP WITH THE IDEA TO LITERALLY, DRAG AN INDIVIDUAL TO DEATH WHEN TIED TO THE BACK OF A TRUCK UNTIL THE BODY IS DISMEMBERED TO THEIR SATISFACTION? WHY DID WE RE-ELECT A PRESIDENT THAT WOULD BE HEARD USING THE TERM "BRING IT ON" AS A RESPONSE TO THE IMPENDING DOOM OF WAR IN THE MIDDLE EAST? WHY DID WE RE-ELECT AND CHOOSE TO FOLLOW A PRESIDENT WE ARE NOW ACCUSING TO BE THE HEAVY IN NOT ACTING IN A PROPER "COMMANDER-IN-CHIEF" POSITION, WHEN A CALL OF AID TO VICTIMS OF HURRICANE KATRINA WAS MADE IN THE GULF AREA, HERE IN THE U.S. AND NOT THE GULF AREA ACROSS THE WORLD IN THE IRAQI AREA?

(OVER)

IT IS APRIL 18, 2006, AS I COMPLETE THE AFTERWORDS FOR "RHYME, REASON AND REVERENCE" BY REMEMBERING THE VERY GOOD SENSE MESSAGES I RECEIVED WHEN I WATCHED MOVIES, OF TODAY, SUCH AS "THE LION KING" AND THE "SHREK". SOMEONE HAS COINED THE PHRASE, "YOU COULD LEARN A LOT FROM A DUMMY". BUT, TODAY, WHERE DO WE GO TO FIND THE DUMMIES, YALE, PRINCETON, COLUMBIA, HOWARD, TULANE MOOREHOUSE OR U.C.L.A.?

WE FIND THE SAME "STUFF" WHEREEVER WE LOOK, TODAY. THE ANSWER, AS FAR AS I AM CONCERNED, IS THERE IS NO ANSWER, BECAUSE THERE IS NO QUESTION. DO WE DARE QUESTION THE ABSOLUTE AUTHORITY OF ONE THAT HAS NO COMPETITION AND, THUS, NO COMPARISON IN MIGHT, STRENGTH, POWER AND MAJESTY THAT ANYONE OF US MIGHT HOPE TO CONQUER AS HE PLACES THE SUN TO SHINE, THE RAIN TO FALL, THE NIGHT TO COVER, THE STARS TO LIGHT, AS WE, DAY AFTER DAY AFTER DAY, RISE, ONLY TO FALL, ONLY TO RISE AND FALL, AGAIN. DO WE DARE QUESTION A MASTER OF US, ALL? NO, WE DON'T, AS WE CONTINUE THE DILEMMA OF MAN THAT IS AS OLD AS THE HILLS THAT WE ALL YIELD AND SURRENDER TO IN EACH OUR OWN WAY.

IT MATTERS, NOT THAT WE, OBVIOUSLY, CAN'T DECIDE WHICH FIVE LETTER WORD TO PAY ALLEGIANCE; SATAN, JESUS OR MONEY. WHAT DOES MATTER IS THAT WE UNDERSTAND THAT WHILE NONE OF US ASKED OR GAVE HIS PERMISSION TO BE HERE ON EARTH, IN THIS WORLD, WE ARE HERE AND THERE IS NOTHING MORE WE CAN SAY OR DO TO CHANGE THAT AS WE CONTINUE TO OFFER OUR BEST TO EACH OTHER.

BIBLIOGRAPHY

NELSON-REGENCY PUBLISHERS-KJV
COPYRIGHT 1990-USA THOMAS NELSON, INC.

STAR JONES FOR THE PEOPLE
STARLET JONES

THE LAST DAYS OF THE LATE GREAT STATE
OF CALIFORNIA BY CURT GENTRY
COPYRIGHT 1968 CURT GENTRY
G.P. PUTNAM'S SONS NEW YORK, PUBLISHER

THE WORD AMONG US 2005

GROWING UP SOUTHERN BY CHRIS MAYFIELD
COPYRIGHT 1976 CHRIS MAYFIELD

FIFTY GREATEST HYMNS

LOVE SONGS

LUTHER VANDROSS

VANESSA WILLIAMS

LIONEL RICHIE

ELTON JOHN

MERRIAM - WEBSTER
FEDERAL STREET PRESS
COPYRIGHT 2000
MERRIAM - WEBSTER, INC.

THE MIDDLE EAST

BARBARA JORDAN BY BARBARA JORDAN

THE IMPORTANCE OF UNDERSTANDING

MY LIFE
COPYRIGHT 2004 WILLIAM J. CLINTON

MILLIONS MORE MOVEMENT
7400 SOUTH STONEY ISLAND AVENUE
CHICAGO, IL 60649

JIM REEVES

AMY GRANT

JOHN LEGEND

KENNY ROGERS

KOOL AND THE GANG

SHE TOOK A VILLAGE

THE JEFFERSON WAY

POPE JOHN PAUL II:
THE LIFE OF KAROL WOTYLA

LOUISIANA TERRITORY BY
JOHN DAVENPORT
COPYRIGHT 1960 JOHN DAVENPORT
CHELSEA HOUSE PUBLISHERS PHILADELPHIA,
PENNSYLVANIA

DISCOVERY HOUSE PUBLISHERS

WORDS NOTED

ZEITGEIST
GAFFES
PILLORING
ACERBIC
RAPACIOUS
TITULAR
JATWA

WORLD HISTORY - THE HUMAN EXPERIENCE
BY MOUNIR FARAH AND ANDREA KARLS
McMILLIAN/McGRAW-HILL
LAKE FOREST, ILLINOIS
COPYRIGHT 1992 GLENCOE DIVISION OF
McMILLIAN/McGRAW-HILL
COPYRIGHT 1990, 1983 by MERRILL PUB. CO.
PRINTED IN THE USA

THE NEWS STAR
MONROE, LOUISIANA

THE FREE PRESS
MONROE, LOUISIANA

THE WORDS OF RHYME, REASON AND REVERENCE ARE, LIKE ONE'S LIFE PAST, PRESENT AND FUTURE, SHOULD BE WITH UNDERSTANDING, PURPOSE AND INTENT. RHYME IS LIKE A FAMILIAR PATHWAY, REASON LIKE A MUCH USED AVENUE AND REVERENCE, A HIGHWAY TO HEAVEN. WHATEVER WAY YOU TRAVEL, BACK ALLEY, NUMBERED STREET OR PAVED ROAD, MAY IT CONTINUE TO BE ONE OF BLESSING AND PROSPERITY.

YOURS,

THE AUTHOR

R

www.ingramcontent.com/pod-product-compliance
Ingram Content Group UK Ltd.
Pitfield, Milton Keynes, MK11 3LW, UK
UKHW041848190726
13854UKWH00002B/769

9 781425 102883